HEALING
SECRETS OF THE
NATIVE
AMERICANS

HEALING
SECRETS OF THE
NATIVE
AMERICANS

•

**Herbs, Remedies and
Practices that Restore the Body,
Refresh the Mind and
Rebuild the Spirit**

•

PORTER SHIMER

BLACK DOG
& LEVENTHAL
PUBLISHERS
NEW YORK

Published by
Black Dog & Leventhal Publishers, Inc.
151 West 19th Street
New York, NY 10011

Distributed by
Workman Publishing Company
708 Broadway
New York, NY 10003

Manufactured in China

Cover and interior design by Sheila Hart Design, Inc.

ISBN: 1-57912-393-7

H G F E D C B A

Library of Congress Cataloging-in-Publication Data available on file.

C O N T E N T S

DOCTORS OF THE EARTH

Every day we're surrounded by powerful remedies that go unnoticed. For example, when we start paying attention, we can find hundreds of different "weeds"— in fields, along roadways and railroad tracks, or even in our own backyards—that are capable of performing wonders for our health.

For the first inhabitants of this continent, the Native Americans, nature was their pharmacy. They were on a first-name basis with hundreds of healing plants, grasses, and herbs. Native Americans also recognized the healing powers within their own bodies and treated them with great respect. They felt that the power to heal was a gift entrusted to them by the Creator and believed that human power and strength came from Mother Earth and all living things.

There's no question that advances in medical science have had a tremendous impact on our lives. People are living longer, healthier lives than ever before. However, some of the benefits of modern medicines may be offset by their costs. Modern drugs are expensive, not just in dollars, but possibly in terms of our long-term health. That's because, as effective as drugs can be, most work by forcing the body to respond in certain ways, rather than by calling upon the body's own natural healing powers. Using drugs can put the body in a passive, dependent, and ultimately weakened state.

Consider what happens when you have an infection. The modern approach is to take an antibiotic, which kills the bacteria that is making you sick. In the short run this is a sensible solution, but the body is exposed to billions of bacteria every day. In the long term, it's a losing battle. Antibiotics, although vital for fighting some infections, are only a temporary defense. They don't help the body strengthen its own defenses and resist future infections.

Native healers took an entirely different approach. The best remedies, in their view, were those that empowered the body to take care of itself, rather than merely providing temporary support. They also deeply believed in a spiritual component to healing—that prayer, visualization, and a variety of healing ceremonies strengthened the body as well as the mind and emotions, making recovery much easier.

Today, an increasing number of mainstream practitioners are supporting this mind-body connection. It's taken hundreds of years, but the wisdom and experience of Native Americans are now on the cutting edge of modern medical care. Indeed, the recent surge in "alternative" healing methods and the use of prayer to heal harkens back to Native American methods: herbs and other so-called "natural" remedies, visualization, meditation, and more.

Many people are surprised to learn how sophisticated Native Americans really were. Often, history presents these intelligent, intuitive people in a very limited light. Although it's true that Native Americans were gifted hunters, tool-makers, and warriors, their gifts were more wide-ranging than that. Until recently, little has been said of their impressive talents as healers.

Among the early colonists, Native Americans were well-known for seemingly miraculous healing feats, yet historians recorded few of these stories, probably because of racial prejudice and the belief that Native Americans were "savages."

Still, stories of Native American medical prowess continued to circulate by word of mouth and were recorded in colonial diaries and journals. Today, we're able to read first-hand accounts from the earliest settlers about what the Native Americans were able to achieve.

In 1650, the Dutch explorer Adrian van der Donck wrote of the high regard early settlers had for Native American healers: "The Indians know how to cure very dangerous and perilous wounds and sores by roots, leaves, and other little things."

Later, in 1714, John Lawson wrote in his *History of North Carolina*: "Among all the discoveries of America by the French and Spaniards, I wonder why none of them was so kind to the world as to have kept a catalog of the illnesses they found the natives able to cure."

Even physicians of the time were impressed. During a meeting of the Philadelphia Medical Society in the winter of 1798, Dr. Benjamin S. Barton, a University of Pennsylvania botanist and medical professor, said: "These people, although destitute of the lights of science, have discovered the properties of some of the most inestimable medicines with which we are acquainted today."

For their part, the Native Americans were very aware of the importance of their medical gifts. After all, life at that time was rugged and difficult, and they recognized that their survival depended on knowledge of the natural world. "The Indians," wrote the French explorer Jean-Bernard Boss in 1762, "value their medicinal herbs more than all the gold of Mexico or Peru."

These earliest inhabitants of the North American continent were far ahead of their time, not just in their use of medicinal plants, but also in the way they lived. At a time when bathing was considered a dangerous practice, for example, the Native Americans would plunge into frigid water in the coldest weather to cleanse their bodies. They were strong and fit, and their physical endurance amazed the Europeans. According to one early account, "These people are a robust and vigorous sort, of a sanguine temperament, admirable complexion and unacquainted with a great many of the diseases that afflict the Europeans."

The bottom line? Early Native Americans were living proof that their way of life was health-giving, largely due to the power of the health secrets you'll find in this book. In these pages you'll discover how the Native Americans used herbs to heal wounds and treat illnesses, and as everyday tonics to maintain their vitality and strength. You'll also learn how they combined spirituality with sound herbal medicine by using meditative techniques, rituals, dance, and music to achieve good health.

Although a fairly complete guide to Native American healing, this book represents only a fraction of the vast number of healing methods and substances the Native Americans used every day. There were some 500 tribes in North America before the arrival of the European settlers, and each had its own ceremonies, practices, and beliefs. Often, tribes shared their knowledge of healing herbs or methods with each other. The remedies you'll find here were among the most widespread. They are also the remedies that are the easiest to adapt for our use today, as well as those modern science has found to be the most effective.

The spiritual component of Native American healing has made studying their methods difficult for scientists at times—difficult to measure and difficult to fully understand. In the Native American view, health was more than just a physical state; it also depended on a person's inner harmony with the powers of nature. Native Americans believed that failing to show adequate respect for Mother Earth and the powers that created her could take a toll on physical health. In his book *American Indian Medicine*, historian Virgil J. Vogel notes that this approach to health "operates for the most part in a realm of reality totally foreign to the Western mind."

Perhaps it's less foreign than it used to be. More and more people today have begun to understand and appreciate so-called "alternative" systems of healing, and science is backing them up. Consider dream therapy. Commonly used among Native Americans to ease hidden emotional turmoil, it's very similar to methods used by modern psychologists. The rhythmic chants and musical rituals of Native Americans have much in common with hypnotic techniques used today. In addition, the sweat lodges used by these native people were the forerunners of the steam rooms, saunas, and whirlpool baths in today's health clubs and medical facilities.

Native Americans are perhaps best known for their understanding of the healing powers of plants, another area in which they were far ahead of their time. Medicinal herbs are now a billion-dollar business. Millions of Americans use herbs, and an increasing number of physicians are recommending them for their patients. Scientists have discovered in laboratories what Native Americans learned thousands of years ago—that within the world of plants is a vast natural pharmacy. Many of the drugs we use today contain ingredients nearly identical to those found in nature. In fact, many of our drugs are simply synthetic versions of herbal extracts that Native Americans used with great success. Aspirin, for example, which continues to amaze doctors with its effectiveness and versatility, is chemically similar to pain-killing compounds found in the bark of the willow tree. Drugs used to treat conditions such as diabetes and heart disease also have their origins in Native American herbal expertise. According to Virgil J. Vogel, "Even in comparatively recent times, Indian discoveries have helped open new frontiers in medical history."

Here's how to use this book most effectively to bring these discoveries into your own life. First, look under individual headings in chapter 3, "The Native American Pharmacy," to find descriptions of traditional Native American uses for a wide variety of herbs and healing practices. These are provided for their historical interest, along with any current scientific findings that generally support their effectiveness. Then, in chapter 4, "Making It Work for You," you'll discover how to apply Native American healing knowledge to your own health concerns today. Common ailments are listed alphabetically, and many of these traditional remedies have been adapted for use at home to ease symptoms or to speed healing. Of course, none of these remedies should replace prompt and appropriate treatment by a physician or other health care provider, so check with your doctor first.

The story of Native American healing is more than just fascinating. It offers a system for healing that's as useful and practical for many health problems today as it was in the past. There's a lot more medicine in nature than most of us realize. From the antibacterial action of the mint in your garden to the muscle-soothing relaxation of massage to the stress-relieving properties of a golden sunrise—the power to control physical and emotional health is very much in your hands. Here may you find a beginning.

THE
HEALING
SPIRIT

The philosophy that underlies all Native American healing techniques—herbal, physical, and spiritual—is really very simple. In order to live healthfully, people must learn to live in harmony with the world around them. In a sense, the Native Americans were the first ecologists. They wanted their relationship with Mother Earth to be as harmonious as possible because they believed that only when they lived in harmony with the earth would they achieve spiritual peace, which was essential for good health.

It's become clear in recent years that they were on to something. Research has shown that our emotional well-being has an enormous impact on physical health. According to Lewis Mehl-Madrona, M.D.,

Medical Director of the Center for Complementary Medicine at the University of Pittsburgh Medical Center and author of *Coyote Medicine*, "When we are in harmony with the earth and the people around us, our cells are in harmony within us. It's disharmony that creates cellular degeneration and disease."

The Native Americans discovered ways of living in harmony with Mother Earth, despite the hardships she sent their way. They dedicated themselves to holding all aspects of their environment, including wild animals and inclement weather, in the highest regard. When they killed a bear, for example, they made a necklace of its claws, which was worn by the warrior to honor the animal's courage and strength. After any successful hunt, they always left gifts such as small pouches of tobacco to express their sincere thanks to Mother Earth. They treated plants the same way. Whether they harvested plants for medicine or food, they always did so with profound respect. It was their way of showing gratitude for the generosity of the Great Spirit, which they believed was responsible for all living things.

They believed that a failure to live in harmony with Mother Nature—by not giving sufficient thanks for successful hunts and harvests, for example—would have dire consequences. According to one historian, "An Indian who hunted animals or gathered herbs must always sing the necessary songs or prayers, or offer gifts of tobacco to the spirits of the animals or plants, as failure to do so might lead to illness or bad luck."

Just a few decades ago, this spiritual approach to nature and the environment sounded strange to modern ears. However, Americans have begun to see the wisdom in the *holistic* approach. The modern phrase "what goes around comes around" shows how much we've come to understand and appreciate the Native American way of living.

HEALTH AS A FAMILY AFFAIR

It's impossible to exaggerate the Native American belief in the interconnectedness of human beings and nature. They looked at all living things, as well as certain physical aspects of nature, such as rivers, mountains, and weather, as relatives—all members of one big and at least potentially happy family. "We share our breath with all that is visible—the deer, bear, hawk, snake, tree and shark," writes Native American psychotherapist Robert Blackwolf Jones. A similar sentiment is expressed by the Native American philosopher Chief Seattle, who wrote: "Man did not weave the web of life, he is merely a strand in it, such that whatever he does to the web, he does to himself."

The Native Americans believed that sickness was often caused by a bad relationship with certain aspects of nature. Although some types of injuries, like snake bites and wounds, had obvious causes, it was harder to explain internal illnesses. The Native Americans felt that "invisible" illnesses were most likely to be caused by the angry spirits of animals, who were taking revenge for insults they received in life. According to historian William Corlett, "An animal ghost will cause trouble if respect is not shown to its body after it has been killed."

Because the Native Americans believed that humans and nature were intimately entwined, almost any thought or action, if it showed disrespect to nature, could have harmful consequences. Spitting on a fire, for example, could anger the spirits and result in illness.

Nature wasn't always viewed with fear, of course. Just as the spirits of animals and other aspects of nature could be harmful when they were angered, they also could be helpful when they were pleased. The Native Americans believed, for example, that herbs and even the organs of animals were full of tremendous healing powers. They also called on the spirits of animals for assistance during their many healing ceremonies.

Different animals were thought to have unique personalities and attributes, such as cunning, intelligence, and strength. Native Americans would call on individual animal spirits during healing ceremonies, asking each in turn to share its unique gifts with the person being healed.

Today, of course, doctors are unlikely to recommend calling on the spirits of eagles and bears to stabilize blood sugar or relieve arthritis, but they're very aware of the power of nature to heal or harm—depending on how it's treated. Excessive exposure to sunlight, for example, can cause cancer, but when the sun is used appropriately (about 15 minutes exposure daily) it helps the body produce vitamin D, essential for strong bones. The foods we eat are filled with nutrients, such as vitamin A, iron, folate, and sodium. In the proper amounts, each of these nutrients is essential to life; in excess, all of them can be harmful.

Because harmony and balance are the keys to health, who could not benefit from taking a lesson from the Native Americans? The place to start is by treating the world around us with the utmost respect. According to Robert Blackwolf Jones, "It's time we climbed down from the lonely pedestal we have created for ourselves and recognize our place alongside our fellow inhabitants."

HEALING WITH KINDNESS

The Native Americans had great reverence not just for the natural world, but for human relationships as well. "An Indian's wealth is measured not by what he possesses, but rather what he gives away," says Robert Blackwolf Jones. "For life to be rich and full, we must give as well as take."

When Native Americans celebrated a birthday, for example, the honoree wasn't lavished with gifts. Rather, he was expected to give his guests presents to honor them for attending. Giving to others, they recognized, was an essential part of living because it brings peace of mind as well as health—gifts that money can't buy.

The Native Americans believed that disease was often caused by what they referred to as "soul loss." This occurred when people abandoned their spiritually generous ways for traits such as selfishness, dishonesty, and despair. The *Encyclopedia of Native American Healing* explains that soul loss could result in a "deterioration in health and strength." Unless the soul was returned to the body, death was sure to follow.

These beliefs may sound strange today, but research has shown that the body does suffer when we hold "negative" thoughts and attitudes. This is why highly aggressive people with "type A" personalities are more likely to suffer heart attacks than calmer, more accepting souls. "Feelings of spiritual emptiness generate conditions that encourage internal cellular breakdown," Dr. Mehl-Madrona says. "Without feelings of fulfillment, connectedness and faith, the body cannot maintain health."

SPIRITUALITY AND PRAYER: THE POWER OF FAITH

The earliest European settlers considered Native Americans essentially pagan, but that was both inaccurate and unjust, for they were intensely religious. They believed not in the singular God of Christian tradition, but rather in a spirit world embodied in animals, plants, and the physical elements of the earth itself. They prayed to these spirits, gave them gifts of appreciation, asked for their guidance, and appealed to them for good health when ill. Again, these prayers bore little resemblance to Christian worship. They were usually performed in elaborate group ceremonies involving song, chanting, and dance.

"These beckonings to the spirit world often were visualized as arrows aimed toward the target goals of healing and the restoration of harmony between the patient and his or her environment," explains Bernyce Barlow, author of *Sacred Sites of the West*. Native American prayers were very detailed and so specific that even certain vowel sounds were assigned particular meanings, such as wisdom, innocence, purity, and strength. The dances, too, were highly choreographed, with every movement having a special significance.

And how often did such spiritual "arrows" hit their intended mark? Dr. Mehl-Madrona conducts shamanic healing ceremonies as the Medical Director of the Center for Complementary Medicine at the University of Pittsburgh Medical Center and has participated in numerous Native American healing ceremonies. "Native American ceremonial treatment methods are the most powerful I have encountered," he says. "Prayer and ceremony hold a magic and a power that cannot be denied."

Dr. Mehl-Madrona reports having witnessed healings that some would term miraculous: a teenage girl cured of gallbladder disease; a woman saved from terminal cancer; a man cured of cirrhosis of the liver. As a medical doctor, Dr. Mehl-Madrona says, he might come up with rational explanations for some of the shamanic healings he has seen, but he prefers not even to try. "It's a grave and sometimes fatal mistake to insist that every experience has an explanation that avoids the power of spirituality," he says. "To be healed, we need to believe in the possibility of being healed, and in a greater world, and in powers higher than our own."

There is some scientific backup for Dr. Mehl-Madrona's position. Recent studies on the power of prayer in general have found that it can have measurable healing effects— even when the person being prayed for knows nothing about it! These findings merely confirm, Dr. Mehl-Madrona says, that the truest reality may simply be "too expansive and complex for us to understand."

So Native Americans, like Dr. Mehl-Madrona, didn't even try. In their faith, they simply appealed to those higher powers and did so with additional belief in the strength of numbers. Traditionally, as many friends and relatives of the patient as possible would attend a Native American healing ceremony so that the power of their prayers would be compounded for greater effect. This communal aspect of their healing ceremonies was symbolic of the harmony between man and the natural environment that the Native Americans believed was crucial. For them, religion and community life were inseparable.

The intense spirituality of the Native Americans demonstrated above all, Dr. Mehl-Madrona says, that with the help of faith, "We all carry within our souls the capacity to heal ourselves. Modern doctors, therefore, must learn to take their patients on spiritual journeys," he says. "Those who do not will miss out on some truly incredible healing tools."

A great deal of recent research validates Dr. Mehl-Madrona's advice. More than 200 studies show that people who have religious faith have lower rates of depression, alcoholism, drug use, and suicide, and also do better at handling stress. Moreover, these studies show that young people who are religious tend to be less sexually active and perform better in school, and that religious married couples are happier and less likely to divorce.

Dreams—both regular and "spirit" dreams—were an important part of Native American culture. Traditional woven totems called dreamcatchers are everywhere these days, displayed in craft shops and even hanging from drivers' rearview mirrors. Legend has it that the center "web" captures dreams, allowing "good" dreams to pass through and uplift the spirit. At the same time, it traps the "bad" dreams to be dissolved in the morning light.

Although today we often use dreamcatchers as mere decorations, there is a powerful connection between our dreams and our health—both physical and mental. An essential ingredient for health, according to Native Americans, was the fulfillment of one's deepest desires. Psychologists today recognize that all of us have wishes, urges, and passions that we rarely talk about and, in fact, may not even be aware of. They're active within us, but buried deep within our unconscious minds. However, desires do have a way of coming to the surface when we dream. We often ignore our dreams and, according to the Native American way of thinking, we do this at our peril.

The Iroquois believed that a person's innermost desires inevitably would emerge in dreams. Unless these desires were acknowledged and in some way resolved, they would fester, causing anxiety as well as physical illness. Native Americans recognized the power of dreams long before Sigmund Freud developed his theories of the unconscious. Even more amazing is the fact that Native Americans dealt with the feelings and urges revealed in dreams by using techniques remarkably similar to the psychoanalytic methods of therapists today. Patients were encouraged to talk about their dreams and, within reasonable limits, to act on the desires they represented.

Historian Virgil J. Vogel tells of a young Native American patient who reported dreaming of feasts. Her "treatment" was to fulfill her desires by feasting—not once, but nine times. Shortly afterward, her health returned.

Dreams symbolize more than unfulfilled desires. They also represent fears that can restrict us and damage our health in ways we're often unaware of, Dr. Mehl-Madrona says. What we would call dream analysis was and is a central part of many Native American healing ceremonies. By talking about dreams and discussing their meaning, healers are able to help patients uncover and understand their deepest fears. These ceremonies usually are conducted by a "medicine man" (or woman) called a shaman, who advises the patient on how to deal with his fears in the real, waking world. Once a person is brought more into harmony—with the external world as well as with his own soul—good health should naturally return.

"Many people mentally hold themselves hostages and repeatedly terrorize themselves with negative thinking patterns and beliefs," says Robert Blackwolf Jones. Many Native Americans use dream therapy to get to the source of their pessimistic beliefs so they can be analyzed and cast aside—for good.

Perhaps no feature of traditional Native American medicine was as unique or important as the healers, or shamans, who practiced it. The shaman was a person who entered a state of spiritual excitement to encounter the normally imperceptible spirit world, and used this experience to help others. A shaman was something of a physician, psychiatrist, priest, fortune-teller, magician, and best friend, all rolled into one.

A shaman's duties included diagnosing illness, which was usually done by conducting in-depth interviews that included dream analysis. Shamans led ritualistic healing ceremonies inside sweat lodges. They practiced herbalism and administered massage. And, like modern physicians, they provided follow-up counseling.

It was the shaman's ability to communicate with the spirit world that made him truly special. Most shamans discovered their powers early in life as a result of visions they experienced during a deep trance. Once they received this early sign, they would undergo rigorous training, usually under the guidance of another shaman, to perfect their unique spiritual awareness.

Shamans had the ability to communicate with spirits throughout the natural world, including the spirits of plants, animals, and the seasons, as well as those of the most basic elements, such as fire, water, earth, and stone. During prolonged periods of singing, drumming, chanting, and praying or, in some cases, after taking an herbal hallucinogen, shamans would enter an altered state of consciousness. Then they called upon the spirits to enlist their healing help.

One of the most dramatic shamanic practices was to suck an allegedly disease-causing object from a patient's body, using either the lips or sometimes a tube made from a hollow animal bone. Afterward, the shaman would show what had been extracted to the patient. It might be a small stick or stone, or even an insect. This caused the illness, explained the shaman, and the patient's health would return.

It seems evident that shamans had more than a little bit of the showman in them. Some of their techniques undoubtedly offered more dramatic impact than actual healing. However, as most doctors will admit, modern medicine also takes advantage of "window dressing" from time to time. Wearing a white coat doesn't make a doctor more skilled, but it's a reassuring symbol that lends a note of authority to the proceedings. And it may, by making people feel more confident about their doctor's "power," help them heal more quickly. Likewise, doctors today still at times make use of the placebo effect—prescribing a harmless pill with no active ingredients or a simple regimen to follow that somehow makes patients feel better. In these cases, as with a shaman's remedy, it is the power of the sick person's belief in the medicine, not the pill itself, that cures.

In a similar way, Native Americans had tremendous faith in shamans' healing powers, and their belief was powerful medicine in its own right. "People had faith in the medicine, and so the medicine worked," wrote one 18th-century observer. More recently, William S. Lyon, author of the *Encyclopedia of Native American Healing*, notes that "my own fieldwork over the past two decades has documented numerous cases in which Native American shamanic treatments succeeded when Western medicine had failed."

Dr. Mehl-Madrona, who is himself a shaman as well as a respected medical doctor, believes that everyone has within himself the ability to heal. "All the shaman does is bring that capacity to life," he says.

In his book *Coyote Medicine*, Dr. Mehl-Madrona writes that ceremonial treatments, such as those used by the shamans, "are the most powerful I have encountered." People need rituals and ceremonies in their lives, he adds. "It doesn't much matter which ceremony, as long as both the healer and the patient believe in it. To be healed, we need to believe in the possibility of being healed, and in powers higher than our own. I believe patients and doctors alike have much to gain by taking a close look at our Native American healing traditions."

Native Americans traditionally believed that only certain people had the ability to be shamans. More recently, Tom Cowan, author of *Shamanism as a Spiritual Practice for Everyday Life*, argues that everyone has the ability to tap into the spirit world to improve health. He believes that what he calls "core" shamanism can be integrated into daily life, just as we might adopt other practices such as yoga, meditation, or prayer. Shamanism needn't conflict with other religious beliefs. In fact, it can strengthen them, Cowan says. Shamanism simply teaches us to understand and communicate with higher levels of existence in ways that help us deal with the less-conscious levels.

Even though traditional shamans sometimes used hallucinogenic plants, shamanism doesn't require anything more mind-altering than something to drum on or a place to connect to, Cowan says. It's not difficult (or scary) to achieve deeply relaxed, trance-like states that will enable you to communicate with the spirit world. All that's required is getting into a state of mind that will temporarily block distracting interferences such as sounds, skin sensations, physical discomfort, or wandering thoughts. These normally get in the way of higher contemplation, Cowan says. The shamanic trance is essentially a form of self-hypnosis—a state of mind in which you let go of daily concerns and allow your imagination to journey into what Cowan calls "the spirit world of non-ordinary reality."

To experience a mild shamanic "journey," close your eyes and begin drumming with your fingertips—you can use a real drum or just a tabletop or other resonant surface. Tap gently if arthritis or another condition causes discomfort. While you drum, imagine that you're leaving the "real" world by journeying through a long tunnel with a light at the end. It doesn't matter what the tunnel looks like—let your imagination conjure what it will—but how you drum does make a difference. To achieve a trance-like state, you must use a steady rhythm of 205 to 220 beats a minute, and keep on drumming for about 10 minutes, making the sound as regular and monotonous as you can. "This is not intended to be music, but rather a mesmerizing sonic drive for the purpose of creating an altered state of consciousness," Cowan explains.

Don't expect a sudden understanding of life's greatest mysteries. Though that would be nice, it's unlikely to happen. But if you give this exercise an honest effort, you'll almost certainly discover some unusual and intriguing insights. At the very least, taking a shamanic journey is a great way to relax when you're feeling particularly stressed. Whether or not you embark on a full-fledged journey into the spirit world, you can temporarily disassociate yourself from the daily concerns of life.

Native American warriors prepared for battle by donning their best clothing and most elaborate headdresses. They did this not to impress or intimidate their enemies, but to be prepared for their own funerals should they die in combat. This willingness to look death in the face bravely, and even to welcome it, is a theme that ran through all of traditional Native American life.

The early Native Americans did not believe in an afterlife, at least not in the Christian sense of souls living eternally in heaven or hell. However, they did believe strongly in immortality. When we die, they believed, our souls leave our bodies and enter a spirit world where they freely communicate with the spirits of other living things that have died throughout the history of the universe, plants and animals included.

The only way souls could enter this spirit world was to become part of the earth, the ultimate place of origin. In *Listen to the Drum*, Robert Blackwolf Jones writes: "We are all born from

Mother Earth and return to Mother Earth. The next time you get mud on your carpet, therefore, don't panic. You're just looking at yourself in the mirror before your time."

Jones is joking, but his point is a serious one. Our time spent alive is simply part of a larger, eternal cycle that travels from birth to death to rebirth in another "world," or another reality. Death is not an end, but another beginning. Nor is it a state of inertness. It's simply a nonphysical state, one in which we exist in a dimension that's different from the one we're used to.

In his poem titled "The Healing Drum," Robert Blackwolf Jones likens the process of death to that of a tree losing its leaves in the fall:

"The autumn leaves are freed from their branches by the Wind Spirits of change. They dance their graceful descent to blend with Sister Water and Mother Soil where they form a fertile bed for infant seeds."

This gives meaning to our deaths. Our physical bodies die so that other forms of life may live. Our spirits, however, live on forever. Native Americans believed that life in the spirit world was just as real as life on earth—so much so that many tribes buried their dead along with their most prized possessions. They wanted the afterlife to be just as enjoyable as life on earth had been.

Death, according to Robert Blackwolf Jones, "is the ultimate life experience." It allows us to enter an eternal spirituality, while at the same time allowing other forms of life to be born. Everyone should yield to death and die gracefully, he says, because in some ways it's the most noble thing we'll ever do.

CHAPTER 2

THE NATIVE AMERICAN SPA

Even though Native Americans had great faith in the healing powers of the mind and trusted the spirit world to help them stay healthy, they were also star students of the body. They gained tremendous knowledge of such things as nutrition, massage, herbs, and treatments with heat and cold. According to a U.S. Army officer in the late 1800s, "The world owes a large debt to the medicine-men of America."

Today, prominent medical experts agree that many Native American remedies and practices are just as valid today as they were centuries ago. According to Andrew Weil, M.D., a Harvard-trained physician and expert in alternative medicine, Native American healing is not merely a historical curiosity, but a "medicine of the future which must be taught in medical schools, practiced in clinics, and brought to all those who seek true health."

It's important to remember that Native American healing, like modern medicine, encompassed an enormous range of remedies and techniques. In future chapters we'll talk a great deal about using herbal remedies for treating many different conditions. However, first we'll look at the physical techniques used in Native American healing—many of which, though they're now called by different names, continue to be used in the best hospitals and clinics today.

THE HEALING POWER OF HEAT

"Give me a fever and I can cure any disease." The Greek healer Hippocrates said those words over 2000 years ago. Even though he didn't understand the scientific basis of disease, what he was referring to is now a well-established medical fact: Many disease-causing microorganisms cannot survive at temperatures much higher than the body's normal 98.6 degrees Fahrenheit.

The beneficial effects of heat were no surprise to Native Americans, either. They treated everything from arthritis to headaches within the sultry confines of specially constructed, steam-producing huts known as sweat lodges. Sweat lodges were used so often and so passionately by Native Americans that the Europeans attempted to ban them, fearing they must house some sort of demon worship.

It's hard to imagine now, but bathing in any form was considered a sin by the Catholics and Protestants who lived in western Europe prior to the mid-1800s. Bathing was so taboo, in fact, that one Spanish queen boasted that she had never bathed in her entire life.

The cleaner Native Americans knew better. They depended on their "sweats" both for health and hygienic benefits, and also for spiritual rewards. Used by virtually all North American tribes, the sweat lodge came to symbolize a form of rebirth from the womb that offered a cleansing and regeneration of the mind and body.

In the Northeast, sweat lodges were made of willow branches covered with birch bark or animal skins. In the Southeast, they often were dug into the side of a hill or made by hollowing out a large dirt mound. In the far Northwest they were made of cedar planks, and very far north, the Inuit even created sweats within the icy confines of their igloos.

Early Native Americans didn't have electricity, of course, so they would first heat rocks in a fire, then use leather tongs or the antlers of a deer or elk to carry them into the lodge. The lodge was sealed as tightly as possible and sweet-smelling plants such as cedar, sweet grass, or sage were placed on the rocks. Finally, water was poured over the rocks, creating an aromatic steam.

Members of most tribes took part in sweats at least weekly. Afterward, they would often dive into a cold river or lake, which completed the cleansing, invigorating experience. Natural springs were especially valued for such post-sweat plunges because their high mineral content was thought to have special healing value. Many of these springs—in Saratoga Springs, New York, for example, and in Palm Springs, California—are still valued for their curative powers today. Indeed, historians have learned that most of the popular spas in America were originally sites used by Native Americans.

The Native Americans of long ago lacked the benefit of medical textbooks and universities, but they intuitively understood that sweats were extremely healthful, for the body as well as the mind. Once again, they were ahead of the curve. For decades, a water-based medical practice called hydrotherapy, which can be very similar to a traditional sweat, has been recommended for easing nervous tension.

Even though early European settlers found Native American bathing habits odd, to say the least, they were frequently astonished by the results. William Penn told of one man, ill with fever and wracked with pain, who followed a sweat by plunging into a frigid lake. Afterward, Penn said, the man "seemed to be as easy and well in health as at any other time."

For a long time, no one was convinced that these hot-and-cold treatments were truly effective. However, research now suggests otherwise. Because sweats can raise the body's temperature well above its normal 98.6 degrees, they're often able to slow or stop the progression of illnesses caused by heat-sensitive viruses and bacteria. Sweating also rids the body of certain toxins—so much so, in fact, that the skin has been called the body's "third kidney."

In addition, the steam generated by water poured on hot rocks creates negative ions, electrically charged particles that can counter stress and fatigue. Add to these benefits heat's well-known ability to relieve muscle and joint pain, and it becomes obvious that the bath-phobic Europeans missed a very beneficial boat.

The Native Americans put in a good day's work to arrange a sweat, but with modern conveniences it can be as easy as turning a hot shower on high, sealing the bottom of the bathroom door, and making yourself comfortable on the "throne" for 15 minutes or so. Then turn on the cold tap and step into the shower for an invigorating shock.

For most people, sweats are entirely safe, but those with major health problems such as heart disease or emphysema should check with their doctors first.

HEALTH AT YOUR FINGERTIPS:

THE POWER OF MASSAGE

Perceptive healers, the Native Americans discovered very early the therapeutic value of touch—not only the soft, loving touches that convey compassion, but also firmer manipulations to treat sprains and swellings, soothe arthritis, and relieve the cramps of menstruation and childbirth. According to the *Encyclopedia of Native American Healing*, "They knew just how to manipulate and massage and pound sore and stiff muscles. They were skilled in the arts of what is known as physiotherapy today."

In *American Indian Medicine*, historian Virgil J. Vogel recounts the story of a U.S. Army colonel's wife who had severe and seemingly incurable leg pains. She was treated by a Native American who "went into the woods, cut twigs and cuttings of the dogwood, removed the bark, boiled them in water and then used the water to rub the woman's legs. Her pain disappeared within two or three days."

To complement the curative powers of massage, the Native Americans used a variety of ointments, including those made from animal fats, petroleum oil, and plants such as valerian, witch hazel, sea algae, and onions. They often performed massage inside a sweat lodge, especially for treating joint problems such as arthritis. This hands-on approach was its most effective when combined with the increased blood flow caused by intense heat.

Historical records are lacking, so no one is sure exactly what techniques Native American masseurs used. However, most experts suspect that they used many of the same types that are still offered by massage therapists today. These include:

Friction. This kind of massage requires forceful use of the fingertips and thumbs to work out knots within the thickest part of the muscles. It also brings greater flexibility to ligaments and tendons in the areas of the body's major joints.

Kneading. Similar to the motions used to prepare bread dough, kneading involves pulling a muscle slightly away from the bone and then squeezing it between the fingers, palms, or thumbs. This technique increases blood flow within the muscle and helps flush out lactic acid and other pain-producing toxins.

Percussion. As the name suggests, this technique involves playing the body like a drum, using fingertips or the side of the palm to gently tap muscles and increase blood flow.

Stroking. Known today as *effleurage,* this is a gentle technique in which the body is treated to long, slow, rhythmic strokes. Stroking is often used to prepare the body for other, more vigorous techniques.

Vibration. This procedure involves using the fingertips or palms to jostle a muscle. Massage therapists believe it can improve the functioning of the nervous system and various glands, and also stimulate circulation.

Of all the Native American healing techniques, massage is probably the most widely available today. To make sure the massage you receive is truly therapeutic and not of the sexual variety, be sure to visit a therapist with the proper credentials. He or she should be a registered massage therapist, a licensed massage therapist, or a certified massage therapist.

HEALTHY VISIONS: SEEING YOURSELF WELL

Golfers use this technique to win tournaments. Basketball players use it to sink game-winning foul shots. Millions of Americans use it every day just to feel better. The technique is called *visualization,* and research has shown it can lower blood pressure, reduce levels of stress hormones, and generally help people perform better and feel at their best.

Visualization is a mental technique in which people create detailed mental images to improve their emotional and physical health. And Native American shamans took visualization very seriously.

In one type of healing session, they would instruct a patient to use the meditative technique of repeating over and over—

sometimes for hours—a certain key word or phrase. This produced a state of profound relaxation and concentration in which the patient would become highly sensitive to the shaman's healing suggestions.

Using another, more aggressive, approach, shamans would "prescribe" prolonged and exhausting dance ceremonies (some lasting as long as six consecutive days without food or sleep). Often performed at sacred sites, these experiences would allow the patient to enter into a suggestive, healing state of mind.

Once the patient had achieved a near-hypnotic state of suggestibility, the shaman would advise him to imagine the spirit of an animal such as a hawk or other flesh-eating creature. Next, the sick person would visualize this animal entering his body and literally devouring the cause of disease. The shaman would then give a detailed account of another animal spirit that followed, bringing the gift of lasting health.

It often worked, and scientists today think they know why.

By scanning the brain, researchers have found that the optic cortex, the part of the brain that responds when we look at a real object, is also functioning when we visualize, or imagine, something in our minds. What affects the brain also affects the body. Studies have shown that visualizing mental images can activate the glands that regulate our most vital physical functions, such as sleep, hunger, thirst, body temperature, and sexual arousal. Visualization has also been shown to stimulate the immune system, which can help us prevent or reverse disease, possibly including heart disease and even cancer.

The great thing about visualization is that you can do it at any time and wherever you happen to be—and you can do it alone or with the guidance of a therapist who specializes in guided imagery. (Guided imagery is the same as visualization, only it's done with the help of a trained practitioner.) The principle is very simple. Find a quiet spot where you won't be disturbed for a while. Get in a comfortable position, close your eyes, and concentrate on gradually relaxing every muscle in your body, starting with your face and working slowly all the way down to your toes. Once you feel totally relaxed, imagine yourself in the most serene setting possible—a deserted beach, for example, or all alone in a sunny meadow or on top of a mountain. Now, you're ready to begin healing yourself.

Think about what's bothering you. It could be office stress or a miserable cold that won't go away. Whatever your condition, imagine it is a specific thing, something you can easily visualize. You might picture a headache, for example, as a hat that's too tight. Now you know what you're up against—in this case, a tight hat. The next step is to visualize the cure. For example, a soothing wind comes along to loosen the hat's tight grip on your brow—looser, looser—and then lifts the hat and blows it away. Let it happen slowly, and keep the picture in your mind for 15 to 20 minutes.

Are you feeling better? Visualization takes practice, and it doesn't always produce results right away. However, even when you can't feel anything happening, your mind is hard at work, and most people will have success within a few sessions. At the very least you'll experience a great feeling of calm, and this can be as effective at healing the body as it is at healing the mind.

For More Information

To learn more about visualization or to find a therapist in your area, contact:

The Academy for Guided Imagery
P.O. Box 2070
Mill Valley, California 94942
1-800-726-2070

THE HEALING POWER OF
SOUND AND MOVEMENT

For the Native Americans, religious belief, life, and healing were inseparable. Virtually every healing ceremony conducted by virtually every Native American tribe resonated with either drumming or singing or both. Along with dance movements and other gestures, such as the sprinkling of cornmeal, these were actually forms of prayer.

The music and dance were not always soothing—at least, not to the European observer. According to one, who witnessed a healing ceremony performed by the Blackfoot tribe in Virginia in the early 1600s, it involved "extreme howling, shouting, singing, and violent gestures." Another witness had similar observations. "The healers have recourse to the drum and rattle and have great confidence in the intolerable noise caused by those instruments."

Why did Native American healers use "sound and fury"? They believed that drumming, singing, and dance would summon help from the spirit world. They knew from experience that the music could produce a trance-like, hypnotic state, not only in the patient, but in the healer as well. This helped them both get into a frame of mind that was conducive to contacting the spirits. "Drumming was essential in helping the shaman make the transition from an ordinary state of consciousness to the shaman state of consciousness," writes William S. Lyon. "Thus, quiet healing ceremonies were almost unheard of."

Doctors today don't use drums, but they do recognize the value of inducing altered states of consciousness. Hypnosis, which the American Medical Association first validated as an effective healing technique in 1958, has been used to treat a variety of conditions, including addiction, anxiety, and chronic pain. People who are hypnotized enter a state very similar to that achieved by shamanic drumming. In this deeply relaxed state of awareness they're more receptive to healing suggestions.

Apart from the hypnotic effects of rhythmic drumming, Native Americans felt it also produced more direct physical benefits. They believed that when people were sick, diseased organs resonated at a different frequency from the rest of the body. The idea was that chanting and drumming would restore normal vibrations and help the organs heal. "In physics, we call this nonlocality," explains physicist Fred Alan Wolf, Ph.D., author of *The Eagle's Quest.* "It means that actions taking place in one locality can instantly affect actions taking place in another."

Some holistic practitioners today use a similar principle when they practice cymatic healing, in which sound waves are directed at diseased cells in the hope of returning their molecular vibrations to a normal state.

Beyond the effects of vibration, music also has the power to affect us emotionally, as anyone who's listened to a soothing performance of Debussy's *Afternoon of the Faun* can attest. Researchers have found that a variety of sounds can affect the body in different ways, and music therapy has been used successfully to treat stress, chronic pain, sleep disorders, and Alzheimer's disease. It's even been shown to help people recover more quickly after surgery.

For More Information

To find a qualified music therapist or hypnotist in your area, contact:

The American Music Therapy Association
8455 Colesville Road, Suite 1000
Silver Spring, Maryland 20910-3392
301-589-3300

The American Institute of Hypnotherapy
16842 Von Karman Avenue, Suite 475
Irvine, California 92606
1-800-634-9766

NATIVE AMERICAN NUTRITION

Television and movies have given us a very distorted view of what Native American life was really like. Although food shortages certainly occurred, historians believe that most Native Americans ate diets that were surprisingly nutritious—and better balanced than those of their European neighbors. According to historian Virgil J. Vogel, "While Indians had no scientific knowledge of nutrition, many had arrived at the understanding that certain kinds of foods were necessary for good health."

Modern nutritionists would be especially proud of the Native Americans for their reliance on vegetables. Rich in heart-healthy (and colon-friendly) fiber and filled with immune-boosting antioxidant nutrients such as vitamins A and C, vegetables made up the bulk of the Native American diet. Some they gathered wild, such as turnips and yams, while others they cultivated, such as corn, squash, and beans. Their agricultural techniques, including fertilization, were very advanced, and Europeans were amazed by the vigor of their crops.

In addition to knowing what was good for them, Native Americans also knew what was bad. In the words of an early French historian, "They boast above all of their skill in dieting, which according to them consists in abstaining from certain foods they find detrimental." Salt, for example, which was introduced by the Europeans, was totally avoided by Native Americans.

Compared to the standard European fare of the time, the Native American diet was surprisingly lean. About 70 percent of their calories came from plant foods. When they did eat meat

it was wild game, which is very lean compared to meat from domesticated animals. Depending on the tribe and the season, these game meats included deer, buffalo, turkey, duck, moose, elk, woodchuck, opossum, squirrel, and rabbit. They apparently liked their meat well-done, which tended to lower the fat content even more.

Native Americans believed that heavy meals impeded the body's ability to recover, so they ate lightly when they were ill. Pregnancy also was considered a time to eat sparingly. Expectant mothers were warned that "eating too much in the later stages of gestation would cause the baby to grow too large and fat, making the pains of labor difficult," according to one observer.

Although we cannot prove precisely what Native Americans ate hundreds of years ago, historians (and cooks) do have a fairly clear picture of their basic diet. A typical winter stew might have included venison, wild onions and leeks, herbs, and wild rice—a filling, balanced meal that nourished the body and warmed the spirit.

CHAPTER 3

THE NATIVE AMERICAN PHARMACY

The year is 1536. Three ships under the command of French explorer Jacques Cartier sit motionless in the frozen waters of the St. Lawrence River, near the present-day city of Montreal. Nearly a quarter of the 110-man crew has already died from scurvy, a disease later proven to be caused by a deficiency of vitamin C. And more continue to succumb.

Despite the calamity, Cartier had a stroke of luck. Witnessing the devastation, a Native American chief named Domagaia ordered his companions to begin gathering and boiling the limbs of a nearby spruce tree. Fed to the dying men, the pungent tea brought them back to life.

It was another 200 years before a British naval doctor

discovered that the cure for scurvy was vitamin C, a nutrient found in many fruits, vegetables, and native plants, including spruce. Vitamin C is also abundant in the adrenal glands of moose and deer—Native American delicacies. Native Americans didn't know about vitamin C or the scientific causes of disease, but their knowledge of natural cures seemed magical to white settlers—and for good reason. Scientists have determined that more than 200 plants widely used by Native Americans contain medicinal compounds. In fact, some of our most commonly used drugs contain active ingredients found in plants that Native Americans knew and used—the aspirin-like compounds in willow are a perfect example.

What was the secret of these people who, with no medical training in the modern sense, knew exactly which plants to use for healing?

Native Americans depended on nature for their survival, says historian Virgil J. Vogel. They prided themselves on being careful observers. They studied how plants grew, where they thrived, and how they affected animals that ate them. Over thousands of years and through much trial and error, they accumulated tremendous stores of knowledge.

It wasn't only their powers of observation that made Native Americans such competent healers. They were aided, they believed, by an ability to communicate with plants about their healing powers. This may sound far-fetched today, but it goes to the heart of Native American healing philosophy. They believed that plants heal by enabling people to become one with Mother Nature. The life-force that moves through the roots of a dandelion was thought to be the same life-force that moves through us. And this force could be felt and understood by anyone patient and attentive enough to listen.

"The Native American healer gathers herbs with a genuine feeling of exchange from one aspect of creation to another," explain Gaea and Shandor Weiss in their book *Native American Healing Traditions*. "The healer regards plants as relatives, in this sense, calling them 'medicine people' believed to be infused with the same energy as all other living things in the universe."

Absurd? Not when you consider that "our bodies are made of the same elements, minerals, and living compounds that are found in the rest of the natural world," say the Weisses. "For every lack or imbalance, therefore, there are plants that can supply the missing factors."

This kind of thinking could be difficult for modernists to accept, but botanists, historians, and pharmacologists who have studied Native American healing point to clear evidence that the early Native Americans knew exactly what they were doing. Whether or not plants heal for "spiritual" reasons is almost beside the point. It doesn't change the fact that these plants *do* heal, and for reasons that are also entirely rational and can be proved in the laboratory.

Researchers estimate that more than 25 percent of the drugs in use today contain active ingredients either derived from or chemically similar to those found in plants. Cancer drugs such as tamoxifen, the heart drug digitalis, and pain-killers such as morphine and aspirin are just a few examples of modern medicines that have their roots in nature.

Thus, there's nothing magical about the herbal cures used by Native Americans. Their sharp powers of observation and their commitment to passing on this knowledge to future generations made the discovery of hundreds of potent remedies not only rational, but almost inevitable. Today, a lot of modern science backs many "natural" remedies, the result of intense investigation by initially skeptical researchers who became convinced by the overwhelming evidence they found.

Native Americans are believed to have used more than 500 healing herbs. In the following pages we'll look at those proven to be safe, effective, and readily available today. You'll learn how to prepare and use them and for which conditions. Although the remedies here represent only a fraction of the Native Americans' vast knowledge, one or perhaps several of them may be just the healing secrets you've been searching for.

ALOE
Aloe vera

Sometimes called a "first-aid kit with roots," it's among the most popular herbs in America today. Aloe was first used by Native Americans in Florida and the southwestern United States. It soon became known as a skin remedy without equal, and its popularity spread quickly.

Native Americans used aloe to speed the healing of burns and wounds, and also as a treatment for insect bites, fungal infections, frostbite, eczema, dry skin, and poison ivy. Today, many skin products contain extracts from this amazing herb, and for good reason. Research has shown that aloe helps skin cells to regenerate, making it ideal for treating skin disorders of all types. It also may be effective for treating gum disease, acne, colitis (inflammation of the large intestine), and ulcers. As a liniment, it can help treat the inflammation of arthritis. Taken internally, it's also been used for easing constipation. Because the pure sap of the aloe plant makes a cooling, healing salve for minor cuts, scrapes, and burns, many people keep an aloe plant growing on their kitchen window sills for quick relief.

PHYSICAL CHARACTERISTICS

Aloe is a cactus-like plant that stands one to two feet high. It has thick, shiny, pale green leaves, which are somewhat prickly along the edges.

WHERE FOUND

Aloe prefers warm, semi-tropical conditions, but it's an adaptable plant. Now found in most parts of the country, it is often grown indoors. It should be watered sparingly and not given too much sun.

METHODS OF USE

The simplest and most effective way to use aloe is to cut off a section of one leaf and squeeze it to release the thick, gel-like sap. Apply the gel to affected areas of the skin. You can buy aloe extracts, which are intended for internal use, in health food stores or herb shops. However, don't take aloe internally without checking with a doctor. Internal use should also be avoided during pregnancy and breast-feeding.

BEARBERRY
Arctostaphylos

Have you ever wondered what Native Americans actually put in their peace pipes? Mainly tobacco, of course, but also a pinch of bearberry. This herb has mild sedative effects, and it was commonly smoked during tribal councils, possibly as a way of fostering friendship and accord among tribal leaders. Bearberry (named for the enthusiasm bears showed for the fruit) is more than a mild tranquilizer. It's also a potent diuretic and antiseptic. Native Americans used it to treat kidney stones and urinary tract infections.

Over the years, herbalists have discovered many other uses for bearberry. According to *The Complete Medicinal Herbal* by Penelope Ody, teas made from bearberry can help treat a condition called prostatic hypertrophy, or enlargement of the prostate gland. Women sometimes use bearberry during heavy menstrual periods or for uterine or vaginal infections. The herb appears to increase the body's output of insulin, and it may be helpful in treating some forms of diabetes.

Bearberry has many other uses as well. Taken in small doses, it may be helpful for treating diarrhea; in larger amounts, it may help relieve constipation. Diluted, it can be used as a mouthwash for treating mouth ulcers and gum inflammation. Applied as a lotion, it can help ease sunburn and skin infections. Bearberry is an astringent, which means it causes the skin to tighten. According to herbalist David Hoffmann, this mild urinary tract antiseptic is useful for treating some cases of bedwetting in children.

PHYSICAL CHARACTERISTICS

Bearberry is a shrub-like evergreen that grows low to the ground in a thick, tangled mass. It has urn-shaped flowers, usually white, but sometimes red-tinged, which bloom from June through September. The plant develops berries during the winter, but it's the leaves that hold medicinal properties. These should be harvested in the fall for maximum strength.

Bearberry is most comfortable in dry sandy soil. It has a large range, and is found from Canada to New Jersey, and west all the way to northern California.

Bearberry can be taken internally as a tea, made by steeping one to two teaspoons of dried leaves for 10 to 15 minutes in a cup of hot water. You can also use bearberry as a douche, mouthwash, or antiseptic by following the same recipe and allowing the liquid to cool to body temperature.

BLACK COHOSH
Cimicifuga racemosa

Women, take note: If herbs could be accused of sexual bias, black cohosh would be guilty as charged. Dubbed the "female fortifier," black cohosh has been shown to reduce hot flashes, sweating, headaches, vertigo, heart palpitations, and tinnitus, or ringing in the ears—all common symptoms of menopause. The herb has been so effective in relieving menopausal problems, in fact, that some doctors believe it may be an acceptable alternative to conventional hormone replacement therapy.

Black cohosh may be effective for treating other female problems as well. Native Americans used it to relieve painful or delayed menstruation and difficult childbirth—the latter because of the herb's ability to relax the muscles of the uterine walls.

Black cohosh wasn't used only by women, however. Native Americans believed it could also help relieve arthritis pain and the discomfort of illnesses such as scarlet fever and smallpox, as well as a variety of respiratory problems, including whooping cough.

Physical Characteristics

Black cohosh, which is also known as "bugbane" because it repels insects, is a tall, graceful plant with thin, blue-green leaves and long, white flowers that bloom from July through August. Most of the medicinal properties reside in the roots, which are best harvested in the fall.

Where Found

The herb grows throughout the eastern United States and Canada, usually on hillsides and in woods that provide partial shade.

Methods of Use

Herbalists often use alcohol to extract the healing compounds from black cohosh, but it also performs well as a tea when steeped in boiling water. Add one teaspoonful of dried root to a cup of water, bring to a boil, and let simmer for 15 minutes. Drink as often as three times a day.

BLACK HAW
Viburnum prunifolium

Here's another herb for a woman's well-being. Although Dr. John Brickell, an 18th-century medical authority, praised black haw for its ability to heal wounds, it was the herb's ability to relieve menstrual cramps that made the greatest impression on Native Americans. "Black haw contains a number of chemicals that have been proven to work as uterine antispasmodics or relaxants," reports herbalist Douglas Shar in *Backyard Medicine Chest*. "The plant's ability to quiet cramps has been well-established."

Herbal authority James A. Duke, Ph.D., author of *The Green Pharmacy*, agrees. "The bark contains at least four substances that help relax the uterus," he writes. "Black haw would be one of the first remedies I'd suggest to my daughter if she came to me complaining of menstrual cramps."

This plant, also called "crampbark," was used by many tribes to treat the discomforts of pregnancy—a use widely recommended by herbalists today.

Native Americans used black haw for many other conditions as well. It was taken as a tea to relieve heart problems, stomach pain, and diarrhea. The leaves of the plant were chewed and applied as a paste to the skin to reduce swelling caused by infections and sprains.

Black haw isn't without side effects, though. In some cases it may aggravate tinnitus, or ringing of the ears, in people already suffering from this condition, says Dr. Duke.

A botanical relative of the honeysuckle plant, black haw grows as an erect, bushy shrub 10 to 25 feet tall. It has dark green leaves and clusters of small white flowers that bloom in the early summer. The plant also bears small black or dark blue berries. The berries are edible, but many people consider them unbearably sweet.

WHERE FOUND

Black haw is found throughout most of the United States, but mainly in the East from Maine to Florida. It can be grown from seed or from existing plants, which are commonly available at garden centers and from mail-order houses. You can buy dried black haw root bark at most health food stores and herb shops.

METHODS OF USE

The easiest, most effective way to use black haw is as a tea. When using the root, put an ounce in a pint of cool water in a saucepan, bring to a boil, and simmer for 20 to 30 minutes. Strain the liquid, cool, and drink as needed. Because black haw is time-consuming to prepare, many people opt for convenience and instead make tea using a tincture, available in health food stores.

CORN
Zea mays

Native Americans introduced corn to the modern world, and it's perhaps their greatest contribution to our daily diets.

However, corn is much more than a versatile and nutritious grain. It's also been widely used for its healing powers.

Spanish explorers in the 16th century reported that Native Americans drank a beverage made from corn to treat problems with the kidneys and bladder. Historians have discovered that a corn-based beverage was used to treat dysentery and indigestion and to increase milk production in nursing mothers. Corn also was widely used by Native Americans to make poultices for skin ulcers, burns, and swelling, and corn oil was applied to ease eczema and dry skin. Even the cobs were used medicinally. Native Americans would burn the cobs, believing that the smoke would help relieve itching caused by insect bites and poison ivy.

Many of the traditional uses for corn have been validated by modern research. Corn, especially the "silk," has been shown to have diuretic properties known to be helpful in treating high blood pressure and infections of the kidneys, bladder, and urinary tract.

As though in testimony to Native American insight, many skin powders today contain cornstarch because it's been shown to help relieve skin conditions such as eczema.

PHYSICAL CHARACTERISTICS

Most varieties of corn grow six to eight feet tall, depending on soil conditions and moisture. The plant has a thick stalk, large bright-green leaves, and "ears" of kernels covered by a multi-layered husk. Between the husk and the kernels is the "silk"—fine strands of protective material that many herbalists believe is the plant's most medicinal portion.

Corn can be grown nearly anywhere in North America, as long as it gets an abundance of moisture and sunlight. It thrives in well-composted soil and usually requires 70 to 80 days to mature.

METHODS OF USE

Corn is multi-talented, medicinally. For internal conditions, its silk can be used fresh or dried to make a tea. Steep two teaspoons, chopped, in a cup of boiling water. Externally, a corn poultice can soothe minor burns and other skin irritations. To prepare the poultice, mix dried cornmeal with milk and apply the paste to the affected areas.

DANDELION
Taraxacum officinale

It's only recently that dandelion has been reduced to the status of suburban pest. For centuries, dandelion ranked among the most potent herbal remedies. Native Americans and Europeans alike viewed the dandelion as almost a panacea—not just a potent medicine, but also a highly nutritious green vegetable.

Native Americans sliced dandelion roots to make a topical antiseptic for wounds, sores, and inflammation in the mouth. They also brewed a tea, made from the leaves, as a mild laxative and digestive aid. The tea was believed to have diuretic properties and was used to "cleanse" the kidneys, bladder, liver, and spleen.

As a food, dandelion is hard to beat. The leaves and roots were eaten raw or boiled. Highly nutritious, dandelion supplied Native Americans with goodly amounts of iron, potassium, phosphorus, and vitamins A, B, C, and D. They even ate the dandelion flowers, which are rich in lecithin, a valuable nutrient that has been shown to help treat a variety of liver problems.

Scientists have since discovered that dandelion is very rich in calcium, containing 200 milligrams of this mineral in 10 grams (about one-third of an ounce) of dried leaves. This suggests that dandelion may be very helpful in preventing osteoporosis, a serious bone-weakening condition that primarily affects women after menopause. And calcium isn't the only reason dandelion is good for the bones. It also contains boron and silicon, valuable trace minerals that play important roles in the bone-preserving process.

The research is preliminary, but some studies suggest that dandelion may even be helpful in preventing Alzheimer's disease, thanks to its ample amounts of lecithin and choline. In laboratory studies, these substances have been shown to help improve memory.

Herbalists today continue to recommend dandelion as a diuretic. Because it helps rid the body of excess water, it can "flush" the kidneys and bladder, which may help keep these organs free of infection.

Dandelion has so many medicinal uses that it's almost impossible to list them all. Studies have shown that dandelion tea can help relieve pneumonia, bronchitis, and other upper respiratory problems. Because it acts as a diuretic, it may be helpful in reducing swelling caused by sprains or localized infections. Some herbalists recommend daily applications of dandelion "milk," the milky sap from leaves and stems, as a safe and effective way of removing corns and warts, says Dr. Duke.

Dandelion's distinctive appearance makes it hard to miss. Its leaves are jagged or tooth-shaped, which explains its name—the word comes from the French *dent de lion*, meaning "tooth of the lion." It blooms into a single, bright yellow flower, which later turns into a round puff of fluffy-headed seeds that go airborne, like tiny parachutes, with the slightest breeze.

WHERE FOUND

Dandelion is one of the hardiest plants on the planet, as gardeners and lawn buffs from northern Canada all the way to the southern tip of Mexico can attest. The plant can put down roots even in the harshest climates and rockiest soils. Early spring and late fall are the best times to harvest the leaves and roots, which become overly bitter during the heat of summer—but summer is the best time for harvesting the flowers. It's best to get them at their fullest bloom, just before they go to seed.

METHODS OF USE

Because dandelion leaves are tender and delicately bitter, they're prized as a salad green. (As a bonus, the leaves are incredibly rich in vitamin A, containing even more of this nutrient than carrots do.) Dandelion can be eaten raw or prepared by boiling or sautéing. Because the leaves do have a bitter note, many people add a little sweetening. Among the Pennsylvania Dutch, for example, dandelions are often served with a dressing made from cider vinegar and sugar, and perhaps a little bacon. The roots are best when boiled or baked, and the flowers can be transformed into a tender delicacy, tasting something like mushrooms, when pan-fried in butter or oil. All parts of the plant can be dried and stored for up to a year without losing their medicinal properties.

ECHINACEA
Echinacea angustifolia

Echinacea has become extremely popular in recent years for helping to subdue colds and other upper respiratory infections. Once again, Native American healers were ahead of the rest of us. According to herbalist Melvin Gilmore, echinacea was used "as a remedy for more ailments than any other plant."

Paul Lee, founder of the Platonic Academy of Herbal Studies, calls echinacea "our leading herb on the list of immuno-stimulants." What this means is that echinacea can strengthen the immune system, making the body better able to resist infection-causing bacteria and viruses. Herbalist David Hoffmann says echinacea "is effective against both bacterial and viral attacks, not so much by killing these organisms, but by supporting the body's own natural defenses against them."

Hoffmann and other herbalists recommend echinacea for upper respiratory infections, including laryngitis and tonsillitis. It may also relieve inflammation in the mucous membranes of the nose and sinuses. When used in a mouthwash, echinacea may be helpful in treating diseases of the gums.

The healing compounds in echinacea are found in the roots. Research has shown that they contain caffeic acid glycoside, a substance that reacts with other chemicals in the body to facilitate wound healing. The roots also contain a substance that fights bacteria and another that combats viruses by inhibiting an enzyme they use to break down cell walls. Used in lotion form, echinacea appears to speed the healing of cuts and sores.

Physical Characteristics

Echinacea is a perennial that looks very much like black-eyed Susan. It has a bristly stem and large, hairy leaves that taper to a point at the end. It grows to a height of about three feet and has a large, pinkish, daisy-like flower at the top.

Where Found

Echinacea grows mostly in open fields and along roadsides in the central plains states west of Ohio. It's an exceptionally hardy plant that can be grown from seed in nearly any fertile, well-drained soil. Extracts of the herb are widely available at pharmacies, herb shops, and health food stores.

Methods of Use

The heart of echinacea's medicinal powers is the root. The roots should be harvested late in the fall after several hard frosts. They should be cleaned, dried for several weeks, then ground into a coarse powder for making teas. To make a tea, add one or two teaspoons of powdered herb to a cup of boiling water. Let simmer for 15 minutes, cool, and drink as needed, up to three times a day. The tea can also be used externally for treating cuts, burns, and eczema—or as a mouthwash to treat gum problems. Some herbalists recommend gargling with the tea to relieve sore throats.

FENNEL
Foeniculum vulgare

Because fennel is renowned for sweetening bad breath and relieving intestinal gas, it was popular among Native Americans for reasons that must have been social as well as medicinal. It has also soothed coughs and calmed indigestion. Fennel can be used as a compress to relieve conjunctivitis, an inflammation of the eyelid, or applied as a poultice to treat muscle and joint pain. Nursing mothers drank fennel tea to increase their production of breast milk.

Fennel's medicinal reputation has only grown over the years, and herbalists recommend it for a variety of conditions. According to herbalist David Hoffmann, "Fennel is a good stomach and intestinal remedy which relieves flatulence and colic while also stimulating digestion and appetite." According to herbal authority David B. Mowrey, Ph.D., "Fennel is especially effective against flatulence in adults," thus showing once again that Native American healers knew exactly what they were doing.

PHYSICAL CHARACTERISTICS

Fennel is a hardy perennial that grows to about five feet. It has a bright-green, shiny stem and feathery, fern-like leaves. It produces tiny, bright yellow flowers in clusters resembling upside-down umbrellas. The flowers give way to seeds, which hold most of the herb's medicinal powers.

WHERE FOUND

Fennel is native to the Mediterranean region, but spread quickly through North America, beginning in California and gradually moving east. It likes full sun and well-drained soil, and does well in most gardens.

METHODS OF USE

Herbalists usually recommend using fennel seeds to make a tea. Add two teaspoons of slightly crushed seeds to a cup of boiling water, let stand for 10 minutes, strain, and drink as often as three times a day.

To prevent flatulence, drink a cup of fennel tea half an hour before eating. For external use, prepare the tea, let cool, then apply where needed.

Fennel seeds are popular as breath mints, which is why some restaurants keep a bowlful near the check-out register. In addition, an oil derived from fennel, available in health food stores, can be used to make a soothing rub for muscle and joint pain.

Apart from its medicinal uses, fennel is prized in the kitchen. The seeds have a rich, sweet flavor and are commonly used to season fish, soups, stews, salads, and breads. You can also eat the fennel bulb as a vegetable, baking or boiling it until tender.

Although fennel is generally safe, it is known to be a uterine stimulant and should be avoided in high doses during pregnancy.

GARLIC
Allium

If you think garlic is popular as a healing herb today, it was even hotter in the past. It has been used by cultures worldwide for thousands of years, and Native Americans were no exception. They used garlic to treat snakebites and wounds. They prepared it as a syrup for respiratory infections, congestion, and colds—and, in what can only be described as a major medical breakthrough, they discovered that garlic could cure scurvy. Scurvy is a serious, potentially fatal disease caused by a deficiency of vitamin C—and garlic, it turns out, is a rich source of this important nutrient.

In recent years, garlic has been the focus of hundreds of scientific studies. Researchers have discovered, for example, that when garlic is crushed it releases a substance called allicin, which has antiviral and antibacterial properties. It has also been shown to help combat infections caused by fungi and yeast. It's even active against flu viruses.

Among its many healing compounds, garlic contains volatile oils that some researchers believe can help clear the lungs and bronchial tubes of congestion. Garlic also contains sulfur compounds which, along with giving garlic its distinctive smell, may be toxic to intestinal parasites. Long before researchers identified these compounds, Native Americans were using garlic to rid people of worms and other parasites.

In some of the most exciting research in recent years, scientists have found that garlic appears to help reduce the risk of heart attacks. It does this in three ways: by lowering blood pressure, reducing levels of harmful LDL cholesterol in the blood, and reducing the tendency of blood to form dangerous, potentially heart-blocking clots. Studies suggest that as little as one clove of fresh garlic a day may be enough to produce these protective effects.

New research suggests garlic's benefits go even further. It appears to be helpful for people with diabetes, migraine headaches, cardiac arrhythmia (irregular heartbeats), and intermittent claudication (poor circulation caused by a narrowing of arteries in the legs). Some experts speculate that garlic may protect against certain forms of cancer as well.

Physical Characteristics

Garlic plants have long, narrow, green leaves that grow to about two feet in height. Most familiar, of course, is the garlic bulb, which consists of 4 to 15 tightly packed cloves.

Where Found

Garlic is thought to have originated in southern Siberia but is now found in most parts of the world. Garlic does best in rich, deep, and moist (but well-drained) soil that gets plenty of sun.

Methods of Use

The simplest way to enjoy the bountiful health benefits of garlic is to eat it, preferably raw. Raw garlic is an acquired taste, of course, and some people find it too overwhelming. Fortunately, garlic retains its medicinal properties when used in other forms. For example:

Garlic tea. Chop or mash several cloves of garlic and let steep in a cup of water for six to eight hours. You can drink the tea for relieving cold or flu symptoms, or you can use it as a gargle for treating a sore throat.

Garlic syrup. Add a pound of garlic to a quart of boiling water. Remove from the heat and let stand for 12 hours, then add enough sugar to achieve a syrup-like consistency. Some people add honey or vinegar boiled with fennel or caraway seeds to improve the taste. Garlic syrup can be used to ease coughs. When taken in small amounts every day it may strengthen immunity and help the heart.

Garlic oil. Slice or mash a clove of garlic, add about a tablespoon of olive oil, and heat briefly. Then strain the oil and store in a dark, stoppered bottle. You can use several drops to ease an earache.

GINSENG
Panax quinquefolias

Ginseng has been used for over 5,000 years, not just in America, but around the world. Native Americans considered ginseng sacred, and warriors sometimes carried it as a good luck charm. It was as a medicine, however, that ginseng made its greatest mark. Native Americans used ginseng to treat headaches, cramps, fevers, vomiting, coughs, cuts, shortness of breath, and infertility in women. The herb was thought to increase sexual desire in both sexes, which may explain why one tribe called it the "man root."

Scientists believe that ginseng's reputation for increasing sexual prowess is, to be charitable, somewhat overstated. However, many herbalists feel that ginseng does increase vitality, making people feel stronger and more energetic. They call ginseng an "adaptogen," meaning that it helps the body adapt to stresses of all types, physical as well as emotional.

Studies suggest that ginseng does reduce fatigue and improve athletic performance. It also may be helpful for stimulating the immune system, improving memory, reducing depression, and, in diabetics, improving the ability to tolerate carbohydrates.

Physical Characteristics

Ginseng has a thin, single stem that separates into several side stems bearing leaves in clusters of four or five each. The herb grows to between one and two feet in height and originates from a large, fleshy, white taproot, which is where most of the medicinal compounds reside. Older plants bear small green flowers and bright red berries.

Where Found

Due to its popularity and value, ginseng is somewhat rare today. It grows wild in shady areas and hardwood forests ranging from eastern Canada to Maine and Minnesota, and southward into the mountain regions of the Carolinas and Georgia.

Ginseng is usually used as a tea, made by adding a teaspoon of powdered root to a cup of boiling water. Let stand for 10 or 15 minutes, then strain and drink as soon as possible. Raw ginseng isn't always easy to find, but health food stores and herb shops usually carry ginseng extracts.

Ginseng is a very helpful herb, but it's possible to get too much of a good thing. Taking too much may cause headaches, hyperactivity, nervousness, depression, and insomnia.

GOLDENROD
Solidago

Native Americans trusted goldenrod to help heal a wide variety of problems, and every part of the plant was used. The roots were made into poultices to treat boils and burns, or chewed to relieve toothaches. The flowers were mashed to make a lotion for soothing bee stings and reducing localized swellings. A tea made from the leaves was used to treat conditions ranging from asthma and colic to headaches and measles. Goldenrod was also used as an antiseptic, and smoke from the burning herb was thought to revive people who had fallen unconscious.

Native Americans often used goldenrod for bladder, gallbladder, and kidney problems, and it's these applications that have best withstood the scrutiny of modern science. Goldenrod contains a compound called leiocarposide, a potent diuretic. German physicians often recommend goldenrod for preventing and treating kidney stones and gallstones, as well as yeast and urinary tract infections.

There are more than 130 varieties of this hardy perennial. The stems typically grow to three to seven feet, and most varieties have small yellow flowers that grow in oblong clusters. Goldenrod has a pleasant smell and anise-like taste. Some people add goldenrod to other herbs to make them more palatable.

WHERE FOUND

Goldenrod is found throughout North America, usually in open fields and along roadsides. It likes full sun, but can grow in nearly any well-drained soil.

METHODS OF USE

The easiest way to use goldenrod is as a tea. Add five teaspoons of dried flowers or leaves to a cup of boiling water. Let stand until cool, then serve. It's best to take goldenrod between meals, three or four times a day.

Goldenrod is safe, but some people may be allergic to it. Use it with caution if you have hay fever or other allergies.

GOLDENSEAL
Hydrastis canadensis

Herbalist Jethro Kloss has called goldenseal "one of the most wonderful remedies in the entire herbal kingdom." So wonderful, in fact, that the plant nearly became extinct in the early 1900s because it was harvested so heavily. In a single year, more than 300,000 pounds were harvested as news of its healing powers spread from North America throughout the world.

The Cherokee were the first Native Americans to discover goldenseal's medicinal strengths, using it as an antiseptic to treat arrow wounds and chewing on the roots to relieve sores in the mouth. Over the years, goldenseal's versatility expanded. It was taken to treat digestive problems such as ulcers, colitis, constipation, and loss of appetite—uses that are consistent with the herb's ability to increase bile secretion from the liver, according to herbalist David Hoffmann.

Goldenseal has also been used to treat earaches, bladder infections, colds and flu, chronic fatigue, tinnitus (ringing in the ears), yeast infections, tonsillitis, canker sores, intestinal parasites, and athlete's foot.

PHYSICAL CHARACTERISTICS

Goldenseal is a small, 6- to 12-inch perennial with an erect, hairy stem, maple-shaped leaves, bright red berries, and a distinctive light-green flower.

WHERE FOUND

Goldenseal is mainly found in the northeastern United States. It prefers moist woodlands, damp meadows, and forested highlands.

Goldenseal is best taken as a tea made from the plant's roots, which should be harvested in the fall. Add a teaspoonful of dried, powdered root to a cup of boiling water, allow to steep for 15 minutes, strain, and take one tablespoonful three to six times a day. The tea may also be used externally to treat cuts, itching, ringworm, eczema, earaches, and conjunctivitis (inflammation of the inner surface of the eyelids).

GRAVELROOT

Eupatorium purpureum

Don't let the lowly name fool you. Gravelroot, also called "joe-pye weed" in honor of a renowned Native American healer, was held in the highest regard by both Native Americans and Europeans.

The herb derives its unusual name from one of its original uses: Native Americans used gravelroot to treat bladder and kidney stones. It was also used to relieve back pain, rheumatism, stomach pain, constipation, colds, and gout. Because it was believed to cause profuse sweating, it was sometimes used to "break" a fever, especially typhoid fever. The Creek tribe in the Alabama region boiled gravelroot to create a steam, which was thought to relieve arthritic pains in the hips.

Gravelroot is widely used today in homeopathy for improving liver and kidney function, easing the aches, pain, and fever that accompany colds and flu, and for clearing upper respiratory congestion. It's sometimes recommended to ease constipation and painful menstruation.

PHYSICAL CHARACTERISTICS

Gravelroot is a perennial that typically grows from 3 to 10 feet in height. It has a rigid, partially hollow stem. Its leaves, crinkly on the upper side, but soft and velvety underneath, grow from the stem in whorls of four or five, every few inches. Pinkish or purple flowers shaped like umbrellas appear at the top of the plant.

WHERE FOUND

Gravelroot is found throughout most of North America, from Canada down to Florida. It usually grows in fertile lowlands, along stream banks, and in moist, wooded areas and swamps.

METHODS OF USE

Gravelroot is best harvested as soon as its flowers open in the early fall. Every part of the plant is medicinally active, and it's usually taken as a tea. Add one to two teaspoons of dried herb to a cup of boiling water, let steep for 10 to 15 minutes, strain, and drink as often as every half hour for a cold or flu.

Use gravelroot in moderation because in large amounts it can be toxic.

HAWTHORN
Crataegus monogyna

Here's an herb to hold close to your heart. Although Native Americans used hawthorn to treat swelling, dysentery, and internal bleeding, researchers today are more excited by its ability to help cardiovascular conditions. According to herbalist David Hoffmann, "This herb provides us with one of the best tonic remedies for the whole of the heart and circulatory system."

Experts believe that hawthorn may be especially useful for treating congestive heart failure, a serious, potentially life-threatening condition, says herbal authority James A. Duke, Ph.D. Hawthorn appears to help the heart in a variety of ways. It can lower cholesterol levels and help prevent the build-up of plaque on artery walls, which allows more blood and oxygen to travel through the arteries. This is essential for preventing heart attacks and relieving angina, the chest pains caused by a shortage of oxygen to the heart muscle.

Hawthorn is also believed to lower high blood pressure by increasing the flexibility of blood vessel walls. It's even been shown to improve some heart conditions associated with diseases of the liver, such as cirrhosis and hepatitis.

Originally, only the berries of the hawthorn tree were thought to be medicinally active, but more recent research has shown that the flowers and leaves contain active compounds, too. Although the berries are best harvested in the fall, the flowers and leaves should be picked in the early summer.

PHYSICAL CHARACTERISTICS

Hawthorn grows as a small tree, about 25 feet high, with thorny branches and small, maple-shaped leaves accompan-ied by small white flowers that grow in clusters. The flowers appear in spring, and the bright-red berries ripen in late summer or early fall.

Where Found

Hawthorn is native to Europe and Asia, but it now grows in many temperate regions in the United States. It's usually found along hedgerows and amid deciduous (leaf-bearing) trees.

Methods of Use

Because hawthorn leaves, flowers, and berries are all medicinally active, you can use any or all of them to make a tea. The berries are the most readily available parts, however, so most people make a berry tea, using either whole berries or a hawthorn extract.

To make a berry tea, pour a cup of boiling water over two tea-spoons of berries. Let stand for 20 minutes, then strain and serve. You can drink the tea as often as three times a day.

Heart conditions are always serious, however, so it's essential to first check with your doctor before using any herbal treatments at home.

HOPS
Humulus lupulus

When we think of hops, we usually conjure images of frothy mugs of beer and high times. Among Native Americans, how-ever, hops served more sober purposes.

The Mohegan tribe used hops blossoms to make a sedative. The blossoms were dried and put in a small sack. When used as a pillow, it was thought to soothe earaches and toothaches and to help people sleep more soundly.

Other tribes chewed hops roots to make a topical antiseptic for wounds. A tea made from the plant's leaves was used to treat anxiety, insomnia, nervous indigestion, ulcers, and premenstrual cramps.

Modern research has done much to confirm the medicinal powers of hops, especially its sedative qualities. According to herbal expert Daniel B. Mowrey, Ph.D., "a soothing, relaxing calm will be experienced within twenty to thirty minutes of ingesting the herb."

Hops appears also to be effective as a digestive aid because its intense bitterness "stimulates digestive function, bile secretion from the liver and the absorption of nutrients," according to herbalist David Winston. Other herbalists recommend hops poultices for easing joint and muscle pain.

PHYSICAL CHARACTERISTICS

Hops grows as a vine similar to wild grapes, which can reach up to 40 feet in height. Small, yellowish-green, cone-shaped flowers appear in the plant's third year of growth. The flowers should be picked in the early fall before fully mature and dried immediately, preferably not in the sun, in order to preserve their maximum strength.

Hops is native to Europe but now grows abundantly in most temperate regions in the United States and Canada. Hops does best in a rich, moist soil that gets full sun.

Most of the medicinal components are in the flowers, and most herbalists recommend taking hops as a tea. Add a teaspoonful of dried flowers to a cup of boiling water, let stand for 10 to 15 minutes, strain, and drink as needed.

As a sleep aid, it's best to drink hops tea about half an hour before going to bed—or you can try putting dried flowers in a small sack and placing it beneath your head at night. This technique wasn't used only by Native Americans, incidentally. President Abraham Lincoln, distraught by the Civil War, is said to have used a hops pillow to help him sleep.

The one problem with using a hops pillow is that the dried herb will rustle and may keep you awake. Herbalists recommend slightly moistening the hops with water, which will keep the boisterous blossoms a little quieter.

HORSETAIL
Equisetum

Horsetail has an amazing history. According to Gaea and Shandor Weiss, authors of *Growing and Using Healing Herbs*, it was one of the main food sources of the plant-eating dinosaurs, and may have played a role in their incredible size. Horsetail, also called shavegrass, is exceptionally rich in bone-building minerals—not only calcium, but also silicon, which contributes to the growth of cartilage and tendons.

The Native Americans valued horsetail for its bone-strengthening and other tissue-regenerating powers. It frequently was used as a poultice to heal fractures and wounds, and it was taken as a tea to stop internal bleeding. They also used the tea to treat urinary tract infections, kidney problems, and ulcers.

Herbalists today recommend horsetail for combating osteoporosis, the bone-thinning disease that often occurs in women after menopause, when declining levels of estrogen reduce the body's ability to absorb calcium.

Some herbalists recommend horsetail for treating bursitis and tendinitis. The silicon in horsetail may help strengthen cartilage and also repair minor damage. And they continue to recommend horsetail for urinary tract infections and kidney stones, as well as enlargement of the prostate gland, incontinence in adults, and bed-wetting in children.

Although it's not something you'd expect from a healing herb, horsetail has another practical use: because of its silicon content, the herb is slightly gritty, which makes it ideal for scrubbing dishes or even sanding wood!

Physical Characteristics

Horsetail appears in two stages. In the first stage, the plant resembles a small Christmas tree. It's about a foot high and has whorls of scaly, bright-green branches. In the second stage, the branches fall off, leaving a barren, olive-green, bamboo-like stalk about 18 inches high.

Horsetail is found throughout North America, and it's often quite bullish about taking over other vegetation. Look for it along roadways and railroad tracks and in wet places such as swamps and at the edges of ponds, streams, and lakes.

Most herbalists recommend using horsetail to make a tea. Add five teaspoons of dried herb, using any part of the plant, and a teaspoonful of sugar to a quart of boiling water. (Adding sugar helps release the silicon.) Reduce the heat and let simmer for three hours. Strain the tea, let it cool, and take a mouthful or so several times a day.

It's best to harvest horsetail in the fall when the silicon content is highest.

JUNIPER
Juniperus communis

Juniper berries were so widely used by Native Americans for healing that the tree itself became known as "the medicine tree." They used juniper berry tea as a diuretic for people with bladder infections. The tea was also used to relieve upset stomachs and as an antiseptic for cleansing wounds. They boiled the berries to produce steam, which was thought to relieve congestion. An oil made from the branches and berries of the juniper tree was used to massage sore joints and muscles. As a bonus, the ointment was an effective insect repellent.

Researchers have found that juniper berries contain a compound that appears to inhibit a number of different viruses, including those that cause herpes and flu. The berries have also been found to fight bacteria, and research suggests they may be helpful for arthritis as well.

Physical Characteristics

A member of the pine family, the juniper is a small tree, 10 to 25 feet high. It has sparsely-needled branches and small, dark purple berries that appear during the second year of growth. All parts of the tree are medicinal, but the berries most of all.

Where Found

Juniper trees are found throughout North America, even in the driest and least fertile soils.

Methods of Use

To make a juniper berry tea, soften two teaspoons of fresh berries by soaking them in water for a few hours. Then add them to a pint of boiling water and let them cook for 30 minutes. Let the tea cool and drink as needed.

Juniper berries are toxic when taken in large amounts or used for extended periods of time. They shouldn't be used during pregnancy, by those with kidney problems, or by anyone who is allergic to pollen.

LADY'S SLIPPER
Cypripedium calceolus

The lady's slipper flower is so beautiful, Native American women often wore it in their hair. However, the herb was valued less for its beauty than for its medicinal brawn. Native American healers used lady's slipper to treat painful menstruation, difficult childbirth, hysteria, chorea (uncontrollable spasmodic movements), and insomnia.

One historian reported that lady's slipper was reputed to have provided restful sleep to a patient so stricken with insomnia even opium hadn't helped. According to herbalist David Hoffmann, "the herb may be used in all stress reactions, emotional tension and anxiety states."

PHYSICAL CHARACTERISTICS

Lady's slipper, which derives its name from its shoe-shaped flower, is unmistakable for its beauty alone. A member of the orchid family, it has large leaves and anywhere from 1 to 12 large, multi-colored, pouch-like flowers at the top. The herb's roots are the most medicinal part and are best gathered in late summer or early fall.

WHERE FOUND

Lady's slipper is found in the eastern United States and as far south as Georgia and Louisiana. It also appears in the western states of Oregon and Arizona.

METHODS OF USE

Lady's slipper is usually used as a tea to relieve insomnia. Add two teaspoons of dried root to a cup of boiling water. Let steep 10 to 15 minutes, strain, and drink as often as necessary.

LICORICE
Glycyrrhiza glabra

If your survival depended on stealthy hunting, as the Native Americans' often did, the last thing you'd want would be an uncontrollable cough. All the strength, skill, and agility in the world wouldn't help if game could hear you hacking and coughing a mile away.

Centuries before cough drops appeared in neat little boxes, Native American tribes were using licorice root to soothe coughs and sore throats. According to Rodale's *Illustrated Encyclopedia of Herbs*, "although we think of licorice primarily as a candy flavoring, its constituents now are being shown to have a remarkable range of pharmacological properties."

Herbalists today recommend licorice root for such diverse conditions as fever, menstrual cramps, irritated bowel and urinary passages, respiratory ailments, ulcers, constipation, low blood pressure, and flu.

Herbal authority James Duke praises licorice for its healing powers. He says it may be helpful for arthritis, asthma, athlete's foot, canker sores, gingivitis, heartburn, chronic fatigue, Lyme disease, psoriasis, prostate enlargement, Addison's disease, dandruff, depression, and even baldness. Laboratory studies suggest that the substance that makes licorice sweet, called glycyrrhizin, may someday play a role in preventing cancer.

PHYSICAL CHARACTERISTICS

The licorice plant, which can grow up to seven feet tall, has short oblong leaves, small purple flowers, and small, reddish-brown pods. The plant's roots hold most of its medicinal value. They branch off from a main taproot in a tangled mass that can extend as much as four feet deep.

WHERE FOUND

Licorice is native to southern Europe and western Asia, but now grows wild in California as well as in some northwestern, midwestern, and eastern states. It can be grown from seed, but does better when started from cuttings, preferably root cuttings. The medicinal potency peaks during the late fall of the plant's third or fourth year.

METHODS OF USE

For internal conditions such as arthritis, colds, or chronic fatigue, licorice is usually used as a tea. You can also use the tea externally to treat skin problems. Add a teaspoonful of dried, powdered licorice root, or a teaspoonful of licorice syrup (see below), to a cup of boiling water. When using licorice root, let stand for about 10 minutes, then strain and serve. With licorice syrup, you can drink the tea as soon as it's mixed and has cooled to a comfortable temperature.

For a licorice antiseptic, it's best to make a very concentrated liquid. Add a pound of fresh licorice root to three pints of water and boil until the liquid is reduced by about one third.

Rather than using fresh or dried root, some herbalists recommend making a licorice syrup, which can be stored in a covered container in the refrigerator. Fill a baking dish with fresh or dried licorice root, cover with water, and simmer in the oven or on the stove top for three to four hours. Discard the roots, strain the remaining liquid, add two teaspoons of honey for every cup of liquid, and store in a sterilized container with a tight-fitting lid. The syrup can be used to make licorice tea, or taken undiluted, one or two teaspoonsful at a time, to relieve a sore throat, cough, or upper respiratory congestion associated with colds or flu.

Because the compounds in licorice can cause water retention, the herb should not be used by pregnant women or by anyone with heart problems, kidney complications, or high blood pressure. Licorice may cause side effects such as lethargy, headaches, or a rise in blood pressure.

MAGNOLIA
Magnolia

Few trees are as beautiful or fragrant when in bloom as the magnolia. But don't let its beguiling charm fool you—it's powerful medicine. History is filled with reports of successful treatments using this aromatic tree. According to a colonial historian, a Swedish settler with ulcerated leg sores quickly recovered after being treated by a Native American who anointed the sores with a mixture of magnolia ashes and pork fat. "This dried up the wounds which before were continually open, and the legs of the old man remained sound until his death," he wrote.

Other reports tell of Native Americans boiling the branches of the magnolia tree to make a tea, which they used to treat colds, fever, dysentery, muscle cramps, and intestinal worms. More recently, herbalists have expanded the uses of magnolia tea, made from either the bark or leaves, to treat nausea, asthma, and tobacco addiction. A magnolia gargle is said to be effective for easing toothaches, and magnolia decoctions have been used as antiseptics for cuts, scrapes, and other skin irritations.

PHYSICAL CHARACTERISTICS

The magnolia is a small tree, 10 to 20 feet high, with smooth grayish bark, three- to four-inch leaves, and large pink and white flowers that bloom in mid-spring.

WHERE FOUND

Magnolias grow mainly in the eastern United States, from southern Maine to the tip of Florida, then west across the gulf states into eastern Texas.

The most medicinally effective part of the magnolia tree is the bark, which is commonly made into a tea. Add two teaspoons of shredded bark, fresh or dried, to a pint of boiling water. Simmer for 30 minutes, then add water to make 16 ounces. Strain the tea and take by the tablespoon as needed.

When using magnolia externally, double the amount of bark used in the recipe.

MILKWEED
Asclepias tuberosa

It's been said that the best way to find milkweed, also known as butterfly weed, is to find a butterfly. That's because butterflies like to lay their eggs among milkweed's bright orange flowers.

Native Americans chewed raw milkweed root as a treatment for asthma, bronchitis, typhoid fever, pleurisy, and congestion. They also used a tea, made by boiling the seeds in milk, to relieve diarrhea. A powder made from the roots was dusted on wounds to stop bleeding. When pounded into a poultice, the fresh roots were applied to swelling, bruises, and snakebites.

Today, milkweed is most commonly used as a treatment for warts. The milk-like juice found in the stems contains tissue-softening enzymes, which are said to eradicate these unsightly growths if applied daily.

Milkweed is a perennial that grows two to four feet high. It has oblong leaves an inch or two in length and flowers that may be orange-white or purple, depending on the species.

WHERE FOUND

Milkweed grows abundantly throughout the United States and Canada. It prefers dry, sunny conditions and is often found in pastures and fields.

METHODS OF USE

To make a milkweed tea, boil four ounces of fresh root in three quarts of water until the liquid is reduced to a quart. Strain, let cool, and drink as needed.

To remove warts, break the stems to extract the milky juice and apply it directly to the wart once a day.

MULLEIN
Verbascum thapsus

Mullein is another herb that Native Americans used to treat conditions in all areas of the body. To treat headaches, they would place a mullein poultice on the forehead. Many tribes smoked dried mullein to soothe respiratory conditions such as asthma and bronchitis. Mullein also was mashed and applied to swellings, sprains, bruises, burns, and wounds. An antiseptic liquid made from the flowers of the plant was used to ease earaches. In some regions, Native Americans even put the fuzzy leaves of mullein inside their shoes to keep their feet warm.

Researchers have confirmed that mullein is helpful for treating respiratory ailments. According to herbal authority Daniel B. Mowrey, Ph.D., mullein contains high levels of mucilage and saponins, making it ideal for conditions such as coughs, asthma, and even emphysema. Herbalist David Hoffmann agrees, citing mullein's ability to reduce inflammation while also "stimulating fluid production and thus facilitating expectoration."

Mullein also shows promise for hay fever sufferers. It appears to inhibit the absorption of allergens through the mucous membranes of the nose. When used externally, the plant has been shown to have antibiotic and anti-inflammatory properties—which explains why Native Americans used it successfully as an antiseptic for wounds and as a gargle for sore throats. A tea made from the plant may also have a calming effect, according to Dr. Mowrey.

Physical Characteristics

Mullein is a hardy biennial with 6- to 15-inch furry leaves and tall, yellow, flowering stalks.

Where Found

This is an herb that can and does grow nearly anywhere. It can be found throughout North America in meadows, along roadways, and in well-tended gardens.

Although mullein flowers are the most medicinally useful, the leaves and roots also have medicinal powers. For an effective cough remedy and decongestant, herbalist Ana Nez Heatherley recommends using mullein as a tea. Add an ounce of fresh, broken mullein leaves to two cups of boiling water. Let steep 10 to 15 minutes, strain, and take as needed. Some people add honey to the tea, which improves the taste.

The seeds of the mullein plant are toxic and shouldn't be used. Mullein also should not be used in any form by people on anticoagulant medication or those who are pregnant.

NETTLE
Urtica dioica

Here's an herb that was literally a "hit" among Native Americans. To help relieve the pains of arthritis, they would take long sprigs and swat the affected joints, trading joint pain for the sting of nettle's prickly needles. A case of robbing Peter to pay Paul? Not really. Research has shown that the sting produced by nettle causes the body to manufacture chemicals that have anti-inflammatory and pain-reducing powers.

Native Americans didn't just swing nettle. They boiled the root of the plant to make a soothing lotion, and anti-arthritic poultices were made from the plant's leaves. Some tribes boiled and ate the plant—wisely, it turns out, because nettle has high levels of boron, a mineral that can help ease arthritis.

Now known to be an excellent styptic (a substance capable of stopping blood flow), nettle was also used to treat serious wounds. In some cases, wounds were dusted with powder made from dried nettle or wrapped with nettle leaves that had been lightly pounded to release their medicinal juices.

Nettle was used internally, too—as a tea to control internal bleeding and as an expectorant to help clear phlegm from the lungs. It was believed that nettle could strengthen the blood—which, because of its high levels of iron and vitamin C (which helps the body absorb iron), it probably did.

Scientists now believe that nettle tea may be helpful for treating conditions as varied as asthma, bladder infections, bronchitis, gum disease, prostate enlargement, premenstrual syndrome, kidney stones, bursitis, tendinitis, and possibly even hair loss.

Physical Characteristics

Nettle is a perennial that resembles mint. It grows to about three feet in height and has a thorny stem and slightly "hairy" jagged-edged, heart-shaped leaves. It produces small green flowers that bloom from late spring through early fall.

Where Found

Nettle is as hardy as it is healthful. It can be found in most parts of North America, often growing in creek beds, along hedges, and in drainage ditches beside roadways. It likes a moist, semi-shady environment, but can do well almost anywhere it's transplanted.

For internal conditions, nettle is best taken as a tea. Add one to two teaspoons of the herb to a cup of boiling water, let stand for 10 minutes, then strain and drink as needed. For arthritis, don gloves to protect your hands and lightly bat the plant against the affected areas.

OAK
Quercus robur

Mighty in its own right, the oak tree was used by Native Americans to keep themselves mighty—or at least healthy—as well. The Houmas tribe would crush the roots of the tree and mix them with alcohol to soothe aching joints. The Ojibwa boiled the bark as a diarrhea remedy. Other tribes used oak bark tea as an expectorant. Some used enemas made with the tea to ease the pain and itching of hemorrhoids. Even the acorns were used because they stimulated thirst, as Native Americans recognized the health benefits of drinking plenty of water.

How mighty a medicine is oak by today's standards? Research shows that the bark of the tree contains compounds called tannins, which can kill germs and help reduce inflammation. Modern herbalists recommend oak tea for treating sinus congestion and postnasal drip associated with colds. This tea is also used as a gargle for treating sore throats, laryngitis, and inflamed tonsils.

According to herbalist Alma Hutchins, oak tea clears the stomach of excess mucus, which she believes can help the body absorb more vital nutrients from foods.

Physical Characteristics

There are 58 varieties of oak trees, which vary widely in size and ideal growing conditions. Most are characterized by their large, three-pronged leaves, which produce small flowers in April, followed by acorns shortly after.

Where Found

Oaks grow abundantly throughout most of North America. They don't do well at high elevations or in areas that are very dry or rocky.

Methods of Use

The bark of the oak tree is where you'll find the strongest medicinal "bite." The highest-potency bark is harvested during mid- to late-spring. To make a tea, add a teaspoonful of fresh or dried bark to a cup of boiling water. Let stand for 10 to 15 minutes, strain, and drink up to three times a day.

OATS
Avena sativa

Best known today as a healthful breakfast food, rich in B vitamins, phosphorus, iron, and dietary fiber, oats were once considered as much a medicine as a meal. Native Americans used teas made from oats to treat diarrhea. Oats were also believed to help relieve anxiety and depression. Poultices made from oats were used to help heal skin conditions such as cold sores, eczema, boils, and hives.

PHYSICAL CHARACTERISTICS

Oats grow on straight, three-foot stalks. The most edible and medicinally useful part of the plant is its seeds, which are encased in a tough, fibrous hull.

WHERE FOUND

Oats originally grew wild throughout North America, but now they're mainly cultivated. The best place to find oats is in your supermarket's cereal aisle or in the bulk bins at health food stores.

METHODS OF USE

Even though all parts of the oat plant are medicinally active, it's the grain that's most used, often in skin-soothing baths. In his book *The Green Pharmacy*, herbal authority James A. Duke, Ph.D., recommends adding several handfuls of oatmeal to a warm bath to help relieve dry, itchy skin and to reduce the irritation of hives.

OREGON GRAPE
Mohania aquifolium

Although this plant has done more lately to improve people's landscapes than their health, its medicinal powers rank "among the most outstanding of all Native American herbs," according to herbalists Gaea and Shandor Weiss. Oregon grape was popular among Native Americans of the Northwest and California, who used it as a root tea for treating fevers, stomachaches, poor appetite, and liver problems, and as a poultice for infected gums.

In recent years, Oregon grape has been used to cleanse the spleen and aid in digestion. It's also very good for the skin, according to herbal authority David B. Mowrey, Ph.D., author of *The Scientific Validation of Herbal Medicine.* "It has an ability to restore the skin to a smooth, clear condition following any kind of skin disease or other illness that may have dried out the skin or produced sores."

PHYSICAL CHARACTERISTICS

Oregon grape is a fast-growing shrub, three to six feet high, with shiny, dark green leaves that resemble those of the holly tree. It has small, yellowish-green flowers, which give way to dark blue, edible berries that grow in bunches like grapes. The plant's roots, however, are its most medicinal portion.

WHERE FOUND

Oregon grape will grow nearly anywhere, but its natural habitat is in the western United States, from Colorado to northern California and north into Canada.

Oregon grape is best prepared as a tea. Add half an ounce of dried root to a quart of boiling water and let steep for 10 to 15 minutes. Strain, let cool, and drink up to three cups a day. This preparation also can be applied to the skin to treat psoriasis and acne.

PEPPERMINT
Mentha piperita

Think mint and you might think julep, or perhaps a lozenge to sweeten your breath.

Not so for Native Americans. Mint was one of their most cherished medicines, used to aid digestion, reduce fever, relieve stomach pain, soothe menstrual cramps, treat colds, stop colic in babies, and increase appetite in people who were sick. Peppermint poultices were thought to reduce swelling and soothe painful joints. Powders made from dried peppermint leaves were sometimes sniffed, like snuff, to treat headaches and improve concentration.

Peppermint's popularity has only grown over the centuries, and it's among the most widely used herbs worldwide. A number of drug companies add peppermint oil to mints to soothe heartburn. It's also an ingredient in topical ointments that ease the pain of arthritis.

Menthol, an ingredient in peppermint, has been shown to increase the stomach's output of digestive juices, which is why it's an aid to digestion. Applied to the skin, it can relieve muscular cramping and other types of localized pain. Other uses for menthol include the treatment of nausea, painful menstruation, intestinal gas, backache, emphysema (menthol is a potent expectorant), gum disease, gallstones, fever, earaches, hives, nervousness, insomnia, and, of course, halitosis (bad breath).

PHYSICAL CHARACTERISTICS

Peppermint usually reaches a height of between two and four feet. It has violet flowers that grow in whorls and can be distinguished from other kinds of mint by its leaves, which are not as "hairy" as other mint varieties and a deeper shade of green.

WHERE FOUND

Peppermint is native to Europe and Australia, but is very well established in the United States and Canada. A hardy perennial, peppermint does best in a moist, semi-shady environment. You can't grow it from seed because it produces none, but cuttings are easily transplanted. It's most potent when harvested in late summer before the stems become woody.

METHODS OF USE

Ways of using peppermint are nearly as numerous as the conditions it can treat. Here, according to Rodale's *Illustrated Encyclopedia of Herbs,* are some of the most common.

- For flatulence: Suck on a sugar cube to which you've added two or three drops of peppermint oil.
- For abdominal pain: Drink a cup of warm milk flavored with fresh peppermint leaves.
- For insomnia: Drink a cup of peppermint tea, made by

adding a teaspoonful of fresh or dried peppermint to a cup of boiling water and allowing it to steep for 10 minutes.

- For colds or flu: Drink a cup of peppermint tea that includes a teaspoonful of fresh or dried chamomile.
- For headaches: Crush freshly gathered peppermint leaves and apply them as a poultice to your forehead.
- For toothache: Apply a few drops of peppermint oil to the sore tooth.
- For chapped hands: Wash your hands in peppermint tea.
- For a sore throat: Gargle with lukewarm peppermint tea.
- For insect bites or stings: Crush a fresh peppermint leaf and apply the poultice.
- For bad breath: Chew on a cluster of fresh peppermint leaves and stems.

PINE
Pinus

For Americans today, the pine tree is seen mainly as a symbol of Christmas cheer—but pine was one of the Native Americans' most important medicines. They made chewing gum from pine resin, which they found soothing for sore throats. Pine needles were crushed and made into a paste for an aromatic headache poultice. The bark was also used as a poultice for such things as wounds, burns, ulcers, and hemorrhoids. Salves made from pine resin were used to treat sore muscles and joints, and pine tea was a popular remedy for colds, coughs, and upper respiratory congestion. In some cases, the needles were ignited because Native Americans believed that breathing pine fumes could relieve backache.

Herbalists continue to recommend pine remedies, often for treating upper respiratory problems. Teas made from dried needles may be useful for easing arthritis, and pine baths may help reduce skin irritation as well as anxiety.

Physical Characteristics

There are more than 90 varieties of pine trees, but all fall into one of two categories: yellow pine and soft white pine, which is the more medicinally active of the two. White pine is characterized by its longer, softer needles, more gangly branches, and a bushier, less triangular shape.

Where Found

Thirty species of pine trees are native to North America and can be found in most parts of the continent.

Methods of Use

To make a pine tea, pour a cup of boiling water onto half a teaspoonful of dried needles and young buds, which are best collected in the spring. Let stand for 10 to 15 minutes, strain, and drink as needed, usually up to three times a day.

To use pine as an inhalant, put two or three handfuls of fresh needles, buds, and twigs in a large saucepan, cover with water, and bring to a boil. Reduce the heat and simmer for five minutes. Remove from heat, then inhale the steam for 15 minutes by leaning over the pot, using a towel over your head to trap the steam.

For a relaxing, skin-friendly bath, soak three handfuls of fresh pine twigs in approximately two pints of water for 30 minutes.

Then bring the mixture to a boil and simmer for 10 minutes. Strain the liquid and add it to your bathwater.

PLANTAIN
Plantago major

When plantain was first brought to North America by the Europeans in the late 1600s, it spread so rapidly that Native Americans called it "white man's foot." However, it wasn't long before plantain became Native American medicine. As a tea, it was used to treat diarrhea, kidney and bladder problems, bed-wetting in children, low back pain, arthritis, heavy menstrual flow, and respiratory problems such as coughs, asthma, and bronchitis. The herb also was used externally as a lotion or poultice for burns, wounds, snake bites, stings from poisonous insects, poison ivy, eczema, and hemorrhoids. Some tribes chewed plantain root to relieve the pain of toothaches.

Researchers today are more interested in plantain's ability to lower cholesterol and control weight. Plantain has ample amounts of a water-soluble dietary fiber called mucilage, which is contained in the husks surrounding the seeds. Researchers in Italy found that obese women given three grams of plantain dissolved in water 30 minutes before meals lost substantially more weight than dieters who weren't given the herb.

"It appears that plantain produces weight loss when taken before meals not just by limiting caloric intake, but also by reducing the absorption of dietary lipids into the bloodstream," according to herbal authority David B. Mowrey, Ph.D. Some researchers feel that the fat-buffering effect of plantain also may help control high blood sugar levels after eating, and so may be useful for those with diabetes.

Another name for plantain seeds, incidentally, is psyllium. Psyllium is available in health food stores and is a common ingredient in over-the-counter laxatives, fiber supplements, and weight control products.

PHYSICAL CHARACTERISTICS

There are over 200 species of plantain, but the most common is about 18 inches high, with large oval leaves that grow in a circular fashion around the base of several long and narrow stems. At the top of these stems are tiny, light-green flowers that bear a small capsule containing the herb's fiber-rich seeds.

WHERE FOUND

In keeping with its nickname, "white man's foot," plantain grows abundantly in civilized as well as natural settings throughout North America. It's often found along roadways, in meadows, in waste areas such as landfills and junkyards, and even— to the dismay of suburbanites—in well-groomed lawns.

METHODS OF USE

Both the seeds and leaves of plantain have medicinal value. Juice squeezed from the fresh leaves can be applied directly to burns, cuts, insect bites, and poison ivy rashes. The dried leaves can be made into a tea, which can also be used externally. To make a tea, add two teaspoons of herb to a cup of boiling water and allow to steep for 10 minutes, then strain and drink as needed.

To make a weight-loss and cholesterol-lowering preparation from the seeds, pour a cup of boiling water over a teaspoonful of the seeds. Allow the mixture to cool, then drink it down, seeds and all. It's best to take this remedy about 30 minutes before eating.

PURSLANE
Portulaca

Purslane is one of those herbs that's as valuable as a vegetable as it is as a medicine. Eaten cooked or raw, purslane is a superb source of the antioxidant vitamins A, C, and E. It also contains riboflavin, calcium, phosphorus, magnesium, and iron. Purslane also is the richest known plant source of omega-3 fatty acids. These fatty acids, which are mainly found in fish oils, may help reduce the risk of heart disease by lowering cholesterol and blood pressure and by reducing the tendency of the blood to form clots in the arteries. Research has also shown that omega-3 fatty acids may boost immunity and help ease the pain of arthritis.

Because purslane contains abundant amounts of magnesium, it's sometimes recommended for combating chronic fatigue and headaches. It also contains lithium, a mood-stabilizing compound that can help ease depression.

Native Americans probably ate purslane, but they were more interested in its medicinal applications. Juice from the plant's leaves was found to soothe burns, insect bites and stings, and earaches. A tea made from the leaves was thought to relieve diarrhea, stomachache, and urinary tract infections—and because purslane contains a lot of vitamin C, it could be used to treat and prevent scurvy.

Herbalists today sometimes recommend purslane for its cosmetic properties. It's an excellent skin cleanser and astringent (skin tightener) and may be helpful in treating acne and wrinkles.

Physical Characteristics

Purslane grows as a thick, mat-like ground cover about eight inches high. Its oval-shaped leaves, approximately one inch long, are thick and glossy, and are accompanied by small, bright-yellow flowers that bloom from June through September.

Where Found

Purslane grows nearly everywhere in North America. In fact, it's often viewed as a nuisance weed in vegetable and flower gardens. It also can be grown from seed in six to eight weeks in well-drained soil that gets plenty of sun.

Methods of Use

The leaves, stems, and flowers of purslane can be eaten raw as salad ingredients, or steamed or boiled as a vegetable similar in taste to asparagus. The plant's seeds can be ground and added to flour or other foods as a nutritional boost.

For medicinal use, the leaves can be broken and their juice applied directly to burns or insect bites and stings. To use purslane internally, boil the entire plant for 15 to 20 minutes. Strain the water, let cool, and drink as a tea. Some herbalists recommend this remedy for soothing stomach pain, diarrhea, and painful urination, although in cases of bladder infection, don't overlook your doctor's advice, which may include a prescription for antibiotics. Purslane can also be used as a diuretic to help rid the body of excess water.

As a skin aid, purslane has the advantage of being a lot cheaper than fancier commercial preparations. To prepare a skin cleanser and astringent, place a cup of chopped purslane leaves and stems between two pieces of double-layered cheesecloth. Put the bundle in a bowl and mash thoroughly with a potato masher or pestle. Once the herb has been well crushed, add a cup of cool water to the bowl and continue mashing the purslane until all the juices have been extracted.

Apply the mixture to your face and leave it on for about five minutes, then rinse thoroughly. Purslane will clean, tighten, and refresh the skin, and can help smooth fine lines and superficial wrinkles.

The preparation will keep for up to five days, as long as you store it in the refrigerator in a tightly sealed container.

RASPBERRY
Rubus idaeus

Perhaps more than any other herb, raspberry demonstrates that Native Americans could see what modern scientists sometimes miss.

Today, raspberry is officially recognized as a flavoring ingredient only. However, Native Americans knew better. They used the leaves to treat nausea, bowel problems, and inflammations of the eyes. They even felt raspberry could assist women giving birth.

It may be time for researchers to take another look. According to herbal authority Daniel B. Mowrey, Ph.D., "Raspberry leaf is an herb particularly well suited for women." It may help regulate the surges of hormones that often occur during menstruation, pregnancy, and childbirth, he explains.

Herbalist David Hoffmann agrees that raspberry deserves more attention than it's gotten in the past. "Raspberry leaves have a long tradition of use in pregnancy to strengthen and tone the tissue of the womb, assisting contractions and checking any hemorrhaging during labor. This action will occur if the herb is drunk regularly throughout pregnancy and also during labor."

But raspberry isn't just an herb for women. It has potent antibacterial properties, which make it well suited for treating kidney and urinary tract infections, as well as mouth problems such as ulcers and bleeding gums. But any infection in the urinary tract can be serious, so be sure to talk to your doctor before using herbal treatments at home.

Physical Characteristics

The raspberry plant is three to four feet tall. It's a slightly prickly bush with leaves about three inches in length. The leaves are pale-green on top and grayish-white underneath. It bears small white flowers during May and June. Dark red berries that grow in clusters appear in July.

Raspberry bushes can be found growing wild in most temperate zones throughout the world.

METHODS OF USE

Both the leaves and berries of the raspberry plant have medicinal properties, but the leaves were traditionally used most often. To make a tea, add two teaspoons of dried leaves to a cup of boiling water. Let stand for 10 to 15 minutes, strain, and drink as needed. You can also use this tea as a gargle for a sore throat and as a mild disinfectant for cuts and other skin irritations.

SAGE
Salvia officinalis

Today we savor sage as a seasoning, but Native Americans used it to spice up their health. In fact, to them the sage plant was sacred, and they often burned sage during healing ceremonies. Because sage retains its color and aroma even during the harshest winters, Native Americans saw it as a symbol of immortality. This may perhaps even explain the herb's Latin name, *salvare*, which means "to save."

Native Americans used sage leaves to make a tea for treating fevers, headaches, arthritis, and diarrhea. As a gargle, the tea was used to soothe sore throats, sores in the mouth, and infected gums. A tea made by boiling the roots was used to relieve menstrual pain and to help reduce the symptoms of menopause.

Herbalists have found additional uses for sage. It is thought to be a tonic that can keep the stomach, intestines, and other organs working well. It also is reputed to boost the health of the brain and the nervous system. British scientists have found some evidence that compounds in sage may even play a role in preventing and treating Alzheimer's disease.

According to herbal authority James A. Duke, Ph.D., sage is rich in compounds that can relieve asthma. It's also good for gingivitis (gum disease), canker sores, tonsillitis, and bad breath. The herb even can be used to make an effective antiperspirant, as well as an insect repellent.

Finally, herbalist Ana Nez Heatherley says there's some evidence that sage may have mild tranquilizing properties, making it helpful for treating anxiety.

PHYSICAL CHARACTERISTICS

A perennial and a member of the mint family, sage grows as a shrub that reaches about 18 inches in height. The plant, which has numerous stems and slightly wrinkled, grayish-green leaves, puts out pink, purple, blue, or white flowers in late spring and early summer. Sage is best harvested shortly before the flowers bloom. It achieves its greatest medicinal potency between its second and fourth years. Many herbalists recommend rotating older plants with newer ones to assure maximum strength.

WHERE FOUND

Sage originated in southern Europe, but has spread throughout North America for the past three centuries. It grows well in garden settings, preferring partial shade and a fairly dry and alkaline soil, but it is also hardy enough to grow wild under a variety of conditions.

Sage is best taken as a tea. Add two or three teaspoons of dried sage leaves to a cup of boiling water. Let stand for 15 minutes, then strain and drink as needed. The tea can also be used as a gargle for mouth sores, gum infections, or a sore throat.

Nursing mothers and pregnant women shouldn't use sage. Those with epilepsy also should avoid it because large amounts could trigger a seizure. In exceptionally large doses, sage may increase the risk of convulsions, even in people without epilepsy.

SASSAFRAS
Sassafras albidum

Few plants were regarded as highly or used as widely by Native Americans as the sassafras tree. Once European settlers arrived and saw what sassafras could do, news of this exciting plant quickly traveled back to Europe. "This tree at one time created greater interest in the Old World than any other American product, not excepting tobacco," wrote historian John Lloyd.

Legend suggests, in fact, that America might not have been discovered by the Europeans at all had it not been for this aromatic tree. Christopher Columbus is said to have been alerted to the presence of land by the sweet smell of the early spring leaves of the sassafras tree.

Native Americans used sassafras roots to make poultices for wounds and skin infections. Both the roots and berries were widely used to make teas for treating nausea, fevers, fatigue, gas pains, menstrual pain, scarlet fever, and even syphilis.

Used externally, a decoction made from sassafras root has been shown to be a helpful antiseptic. Many herbalists recommend this decoction to ease poison ivy rashes and to kill lice. A preparation made from the gummy core of sassafras branches was reportedly used by Native Americans to soothe tired eyes.

PHYSICAL CHARACTERISTICS

Generally 30 to 50 feet tall, sassafras is a deciduous tree with small, highly aromatic, mitten-shaped leaves that may have one or two "thumbs." It has a gray, deeply ridged bark and a thick trunk that can reach six feet in diameter. It bears small, greenish-yellow flowers in the spring.

WHERE FOUND

Sassafras is found in most parts of the eastern United States, extending as far west as Michigan and Texas.

METHODS OF USE

To relieve rashes or disinfect superficial cuts or scrapes, add two ounces of fresh sassafras leaves to a pint of boiling water and let simmer for 15 minutes to an hour. After the mixture has cooled, apply it to the affected areas as a wet compress.

SQUAW WEED
Senecio aureus

As the name suggests, squaw weed, also called "life root," was used primarily to treat problems experienced by Native American women. The Catawba of the Southeast, for example, used a squaw weed tea to ease the pain of childbirth and to relieve symptoms of difficult menstruation. The herb was used by other tribes to stop internal bleeding and was also thought to be a stimulant.

According to herbalist David Hoffmann, squaw weed was sometimes used as a douche to treat leukorrhea, a condition that causes excessive vaginal mucus.

PHYSICAL CHARACTERISTICS

Squaw weed is a small perennial, between one and two feet high, with an erect, smooth stem. Rounded leaves grow sparsely at the bottom section of the plant and feathery fern-like leaves grow from the top portion. It bears small yellow flowers during May and June.

WHERE FOUND

Squaw weed grows primarily in the eastern United States. It prefers wet areas such as marshes and the banks of rivers and creeks.

METHODS OF USE

Squaw weed is best taken as a tea, using a teaspoonful of dried herb (root or leaves) in a cup of boiling water. Allow the tea to steep 10 to 15 minutes, strain, and drink three to four times a day.

Caution: Don't drink squaw weed tea more than four times a day because it can be toxic in large amounts.

VALERIAN
Valeriana officianalis

This plant may have been among the world's very first tranquilizers. Its name derives from the Latin word *valere*, which means "courage"—a trait that may have been fostered by the herb's ability to reduce anxiety and fear. In fact, many people in England sipped valerian tea to steady their nerves during the German air bombardments of World War II.

Native Americans were well aware of valerian's relaxing effects—on the body as well as the mind. The roots were eaten either dried or raw to treat muscular cramping, intestinal colic, and the pains of menstruation. Some tribes ground valerian's carrot-like roots into a flour, which they mixed into bread or mush.

Valerian is one of the most widely used herbs in the world today. Herbalists recommend it for anxiety, insomnia, migraine headaches, tension headaches, high blood pressure, irregular heartbeat, hives, disturbed digestion, and hyperactivity in children. It also may help relieve arthritis in those cases where the condition is exacerbated by stress.

Physical Characteristics

Valerian is a perennial herb that usually grows to be two to five feet in height. It has a pale-green stem, large leaves, and light yellow flowers that bloom from June through August. Its roots, which contain most of the medicinal compounds, have an aroma that's been compared to dirty socks.

Where Found

Valerian is native to Europe and western Asia, but now is also found in the northern United States and Canada. It prefers damp areas such as woods, low-lying meadows, and the banks of rivers and streams.

Methods of Use

Valerian is best taken as a root tea, made by adding one to two teaspoons of dried herb to a cup of boiling water. Let it steep 10 to 15 minutes, then strain and drink as needed.

Cats are strongly attracted to the aroma of valerian, so don't be surprised if your cat tries to dip his whiskers into your cup. Be sure to store the herb well sealed.

Unfortunately, rodents are also attracted by the smell. It's been suggested that it wasn't the flute-playing of the legendary Pied Piper that lured rats to their deaths, but the smell of the valerian he stuffed in his pockets!

VIOLET
Viola

Valued for more than its pretty face, the wild violet became a medicinal mainstay for many Native American tribes. The Ojibwa are reported to have used a decoction made from the roots of the white violet for treating bladder pain and one using the roots of the yellow violet for sore throats. The Potawatomi used the roots of the yellow violet as a tonic for heart problems. Other tribes used various species of violet for diarrhea, fever, gas, indigestion, bronchitis, headaches, and poor circulation.

Scientists have found that most species of violet, in addition to being great sources of vitamins A and C, contain a chemical similar to the active ingredient in aspirin.

Violets also are rich in a substance called rutin, which research shows can strengthen capillary walls, possibly making it helpful for preventing and treating varicose veins. The studies showed that rutin is effective in amounts ranging from 20 to 100 milligrams. A half-cup of fresh violet flowers contains between 200 and 2,300 milligrams of rutin, says herbal authority James A. Duke, Ph.D.

PHYSICAL CHARACTERISTICS

There are more than 400 species of wild violet. Most are perennials, but some grow annually. They generally reach four to six inches in height, have oval leaves, and small white, violet, or yellow flowers that bloom in April and May.

Violet can be found throughout the United States. It prefers damp, shady environments, and often grows near tall shrubbery and within sparse woodlands.

METHODS OF USE

All parts of the violet are medicinally active and can be used fresh or dried. Make a tea by boiling any part of the plant for about 15 minutes, using a teaspoonful of herb in a cup of water. Or you can make the tea into a syrup with further boiling to reduce the liquid and adding a little bit of honey.

Native Americans sometimes used violet poultices, which they applied to the head as a treatment for headaches.

The African violet is not related to wild violet and should not be used as medicine.

WATERCRESS
Nasturtium officinale

If you already enjoy the spicy bite of watercress in sandwiches and salads, you might want to take an extra helping for your health. Watercress is exceptionally nutritious, with healthful amounts of vitamins A, C, and E, along with minerals such as calcium, magnesium, iron, and copper. Although native to Europe, it didn't take long to spread throughout North America and Mexico, and Native Americans quickly discovered its healing powers.

They used watercress tea to treat liver and kidney problems, gallstones, nervousness, colds, and a variety of upper respiratory infections. Juice from the plant's leaves was used externally to treat skin conditions such as acne and ringworm. The juice was even applied to the scalp in an attempt to prevent hair loss.

PHYSICAL CHARACTERISTICS

Watercress is characterized by leafy stems one to three feet long. It has small white flowers and fleshy oblong leaves that grow in clusters of three to seven leaves each.

WHERE FOUND

Watercress grows throughout the United States and Mexico and most of Canada. Look for it growing in shallow creeks, along the edges of slow-moving rivers, and in ponds and lakes wherever the water is clear, cool, and in motion. The herb does best in water two to six inches deep. Its leafy stems usually protrude several inches above the water's surface. It's also widely available in supermarkets.

METHODS OF USE

To make watercress tea, add a teaspoonful of dried or fresh herb to a cup of boiling water. Let stand for about 10 minutes, then strain and drink as needed. The same tea can also be used as a skin wash for rashes, eczema, or acne.

For a more astringent facial tonic, crush the leaves to extract the juice and apply it to your skin. Some herbalists recommend mixing watercress juice with a little vinegar and applying it to the forehead to get a quick jolt of energy.

Wild watercress should be thoroughly washed because it may harbor parasites. In large amounts, it may irritate the kidneys, so you don't want to use it every day.

WHITE POPLAR
Populus tremuloides

Although the earliest settlers valued poplar mostly as a wood for making furniture, Native Americans prized the tree as medicine. They used poplar for conditions as varied as colds, fever, diarrhea, arthritis, urinary tract infections, general weakness, and loss of appetite. More importantly, they used poplar to treat broken bones, using a technique that amazed early settlers.

A liquid made from boiling the tree's bark was cooled, then poured over the injured area to reduce pain. Then a healer would set the broken bone, at which point a cast was made from poplar wood to stabilize the break. Early settlers are said to have marveled at the success of this technique, which far surpassed their own treatments.

Science has confirmed that Native Americans were right on target. Poplar contains compounds chemically similar to the ingredients in aspirin. Poplar remedies reduced pain and inflammation, which could help serious injuries, such as broken bones, heal more quickly.

PHYSICAL CHARACTERISTICS

Poplar is a deciduous tree, 40 to 50 feet tall, with a light gray bark and dark green, heart-shaped leaves that turn bright yellow in the fall.

WHERE FOUND

It's hard to think of a place where poplar trees don't grow. They're found throughout the United States and Canada, in climate zones ranging from subtropical to subarctic.

METHODS OF USE

It no longer makes sense to use poplar for treating broken bones, since your doctor will do a better, and safer, job. However, you can use poplar tea to relieve the pain of arthritis. Add one to two teaspoons of fresh or dried poplar bark, which is most effective when it's collected in the spring, to a cup of boiling water. Reduce the heat and let simmer for 15 minutes. Strain the liquid, let cool, and drink up to three times a day, or more often to control pain.

WILD ROSE
Rosaceae

Legend has it that when the United States government forced the Cherokees on a march westward from their land in North Carolina, the women shed tears that sprouted into rose bushes. This story reflects the importance of the wild rose in Native American life.

The petals of rose flowers were dried and crushed into powder, which was then applied to fever sores and blisters. After soaking in rainwater, rose petals were used as compresses for sore eyes. The bark of the root was applied to boils, and Native Americans ate the berries, known as rose hips, which are unparalleled sources of vitamin C. This helped protect them from colds and, more importantly, from the serious deficiency disease known as scurvy.

The berries, flowers, leaves, stems, and roots of roses are widely used by herbalists today. Teas made from rose petals are thought to boost the immune system and are also used as sore throat gargles. The berries are widely used to prevent and treat colds and may be of some use in protecting against constipation and problems with the gallbladder, kidneys, and bladder. Even the captivating aroma of roses may have health benefits. Research suggests that flower scents, which are used in aromatherapy, can relieve anxiety, headaches, and other conditions commonly caused by stress.

Physical Characteristics

Most rose species grow upright as a shrub, although some are climbing vines. All roses have thorny stems and white, pink, or red flowers that grow in clusters or alone, one on each branch. The berry-like fruit needs cold weather to mature and appears late in the plant's growing season.

Where Found

Native to the Middle East, rose bushes and vines are found in temperate climates worldwide.

The berries of the rose bush pack the strongest punch, both as medicine and as a source of vitamin C. More effective fresh than dried, they can be made into a tea. First, cut a small slit in each berry, then add two or three teaspoons of berries to a cup of boiling water and simmer for 10 minutes. (You can also make teas using dried petals and leaves.) Strain the liquid, add some honey, and enjoy.

WILLOW
Salix

The list of ills for which Native American healers used the willow tree seems long enough to fill a medical dictionary. Tribes in California used a willow bark tea for treating back pain. The Pima of Arizona used a decoction made from willow leaves to reduce fever. The Menominee of the Midwest made a root tea for treating colic and diarrhea. The Montagnai of eastern Canada used a mush made from the bark to ease headache. The list goes on and on.

There's no longer any doubt that willow fully deserves its healing reputation. It's a rich source of a compound called salicin, which is very similar to the pain-killing, fever-reducing ingredient in aspirin.

In his book *The Green Pharmacy*, herbal authority James A. Duke, Ph.D., identifies 23 conditions for which willow has proven beneficial, not the least of which is heart disease. Research has shown that taking between one-half and one tablet of standard aspirin a day can substantially reduce the risk of heart attacks and strokes. Aspirin inhibits the formation of blood clots that can potentially block arteries and prevent blood from reaching the heart or brain. It's possible to get the same protective effects by drinking one cup of willow bark tea every other day, he says.

Willow tea appears to be helpful for virtually any condition normally treated by aspirin, according to Dr. Duke. The list includes osteoarthritis, back pain, bursitis, tendinitis, headache, earache, toothache, carpal tunnel syndrome, colds, and fever.

Willow bark tea isn't perfect, Dr. Duke notes. If aspirin irritates your stomach, willow bark may do the same. However, you may be able to reduce discomfort by adding a teaspoonful of dried licorice root to the willow before you start brewing the tea.

Willow can also be used externally. Native American healers used the bark to dissolve corns and callused bunions. A poultice made with dried willow root powder can also ease corns. Some herbalists recommend using a strong willow tea as a gargle for sore throats, as well as an antiseptic for superficial cuts and scrapes.

The acids in willow can be irritating, however, so it's important to keep the liquid off the surrounding skin as much as possible.

PHYSICAL CHARACTERISTICS

There are approximately 300 forms of willow, ranging in size from tiny bushes less than an inch high to trees towering over 100 feet. The largest and most common variety in North America is the black willow, which is distinguished by its deeply ridged, dark brown bark, reddish to orange twig-like branches, and long, narrow leaves that taper to a point.

Willow grows almost as readily as it heals. It's found in most parts of North America, the exception being the northern-most regions of Canada. It will grow so vigorously under wet conditions that it can usually be started in damp areas from a cutting.

METHODS OF USE

To make willow tea, add a teaspoonful of dried bark to a cup of boiling water, let steep for 15 minutes, then strain and drink as needed.

Caution: Because willow bark contains compounds similar to those in aspirin, it should not be given to children as it may increase the risk of Reye's syndrome, a potentially serious neurological disorder.

WORMWOOD
Artemisia absinthium

As its name suggests, wormwood—also called sagebrush—was used most often by Native Americans to purge parasites from the intestinal tract. They drank hot wormwood tea for fever, indigestion, nausea, and painful menstruation. They applied poultices of wormwood leaves to relieve the pain of arthritis, and the leaves also were dried, powdered, and dusted on babies suffering from diaper rash. When prepared as a lotion, wormwood was also used to repel insects and to clean wounds.

Wormwood is often applied externally to treat painful bruises and sprains. According to herbalist John Lust, "The herb acts as a local anesthetic and can be useful in relieving the pains of rheumatism, neuralgia (nerve pain) and arthritis."

As more proof that Native Americans were progressive in healing, the manufacturers of Absorbine Jr. include extracts of wormwood among the active ingredients in this over-the-counter liniment for muscle and back pain.

Physical Characteristics

Wormwood is a tall bushy plant similar in appearance and scent to sage. It grows to between two and four feet high, with leaves approximately four inches long and small yellow flowers scattered throughout the bush. The flowers bloom from June through September.

Where Found

Wormwood grows mostly as a weed in the western and northern United States and also in southern Canada.

Methods of Use

You can make a wormwood tea by adding a teaspoonful of crushed leaves (dried or fresh) to one cup of boiling water and steeping for about 15 minutes. Drink the tea as a mild sedative, digestive aid, or cold remedy, or use it externally as an antiseptic for cuts and scrapes, or as a mild topical anesthetic for soothing sprains, sore muscles, or joint pain.

Wormwood shouldn't be used during pregnancy or by anyone suffering from bronchitis or emphysema. Some people are allergic to wormwood; if a rash develops, stop using it immediately.

YARROW
Achillea millefolium

The medicinal history of this herb is as long as the list of ills it can treat. The Greek hero Achilles is said to have used yarrow to treat the wounds of his stricken soldiers. Native Americans also used yarrow for wounds, but that was just the beginning.

Yarrow was often taken as a tea for stomach problems and fever. It was made into poultices for treating rashes, swelling, eczema, and spider bites. Historians estimate that 46 different tribes used yarrow for as many as 28 disorders, making it one of the most widely used herbs.

Modern herbalists have made the list even longer. Some recommend yarrow for high blood pressure, ulcers, internal and external bleeding, liver problems, diarrhea, colds and flu, irritable bowel syndrome, Crohn's disease, bladder infections, gas pains, hemorrhoids, heavy menstrual flow, and problems associated with menopause. It also acts as a mild sedative and can help relieve anxiety and insomnia. A juice made from the leaves can help reduce the redness of bloodshot eyes.

PHYSICAL CHARACTERISTICS

Yarrow grows to about three feet in height. It has feathery

leaves and a canopy of white or pink flowers at the top. It has a pleasantly sweet aroma, but a bitter taste due to its high medicinal content.

Where Found

Yarrow grows throughout the United States and most of Canada, usually in meadows, pastures, and along roadsides. It grows well when cultivated, and can tolerate practically any soil that's not too wet or heavily shaded.

Methods of Use

The most potent parts of the plant are the uppermost leaves and flowers, which are well suited for making tea. Some herbalists recommend making a poultice and applying yarrow directly to the skin. In some cases, it's even chewed to relieve toothache.

To make a tea, add one to two teaspoons of leaves or flowers (dried or fresh) to a cup of boiling water. Let stand for 15 minutes, strain, and drink as needed—or you can apply the tea to the skin to relieve burns, bruises, or other irritations.

CHAPTER 4

MAKING IT WORK FOR YOU

When you walk the streets of any American city full of skyscrapers, expensive cars, television satellites, and people glued to flip phones, it's hard to believe that barely a century ago most Americans lived very close to the land. There's no question that progress has given us conveniences and, in many instances, an easier way of life. What it hasn't given us is a sense of belonging. With every new technology that insulates us from nature and from the human community, we retreat farther into our offices or dens—and farther from a great source of strength and vitality.

The Native Americans understood their surroundings more intimately than we can imagine. When they looked at a tree or a field, they saw food, medicine, life. They observed their world closely, learned its mysteries, and discovered how to put it to the best possible use.

America's health care system is among the best in the world, and the medical breakthroughs we take for granted would have astounded the early Americans. However, this progress has come with a price. Medications that fight disease with microscopic precision often cause side effects that make us feel worse in other ways—and modern medicine often treats our symptoms, without stimulating the body's inborn ability to heal itself.

It's true that Native Americans depended on their healers much as we rely on our doctors. They went to them for medicines and for guidance in recovery. However, they never lost sight of the fact that good health, like the richness of nature, is a never-ending cycle of discovery, faith, and gratitude. And so they watched life around them—and their health—closely. They learned. And they gave thanks for each and every healing remedy nature bestowed.

We, in turn, can give thanks for the healing secrets they have bequeathed to us. There are so many to choose from! It doesn't matter whether you have low energy, arthritis, or a bad back—or if you simply nicked yourself this morning in the kitchen. Hundreds of years ago the Native Americans had many of the same problems and concerns, and the solutions they discovered then are equally effective today.

In the following pages you'll find discussions of many of the most common health problems we face today, along with the best Native American remedies for each condition. Be sure to consult with your doctor to rule out any serious illness before using them, however. And always use Native American healing techniques to complement—not to replace—your doctor's care.

It's hard to believe that natural remedies developed and refined so long ago can not only complement but sometimes even surpass the abilities of modern medicine. However, it wouldn't have surprised the Native Americans. After all, they derived their strength from Mother Nature, and there's no greater power for achieving good health.

PREPARING HERBS

Native Americans' faith in the healing power of herbs was equaled only by their ingenuity in using them. They generally used all parts of the plants, although different parts were prepared in a variety of ways. Herb use also varied from tribe to tribe. Every healer had his or her own favorite recipes and preparations. Sometimes herbs were smoked through special ceremonial pipes, or burned so that the potent fumes could be inhaled, or mixed with alcohol as tinctures, or combined with animal fats to make salves. Another, more primitive, method was simply to chew an herb to release the oils, then apply it to the part of the body where it was needed. Some healing ceremonies called for patients to be burned with the smoldering branches of certain herbs for the desired therapeutic effect.

The most common herbal preparations, however, weren't so exotic. In fact, the shamans of centuries ago prepared herbs in much the same way as herbalists do today. You'll find very detailed information on different ways of using herbs in the books listed in the bibliography on page 174. But for basic use, here are the most common methods:

Herbal teas. Also called infusions, teas are made by steeping leaves, seeds, or bark in hot water. Herbal teas are primarily

used for drinking, although the liquid may be applied externally to treat cuts, burns, sprains, bruises, insect bites, or poison ivy.

To make a tea, put a teaspoonful of dried herb (or two teaspoons of fresh) in a cup of boiling water and allow the mixture
to stand, or infuse, for 10 to 15 minutes. This allows medicinal
compounds to free themselves from the herb and be released
into the water. Strain the liquid using cheesecloth or a coffee
filter—or just use a tea ball—then drink as soon as it's cool
enough not to burn. Herbal teas lose their effectiveness very
quickly, so it's important to use them right away. After a few
hours, most of the healing power will be gone.

You can make stronger teas by doubling the amount of herb,
but that's generally the limit. More than this amount will not
make it more effective and may increase the risk of side effects.

Herbal decoctions. This method is used for the woodier herbs, or
when using roots, stems, bark, seeds, or flowers from which the
medicinal compounds are not easily released.

Put an ounce of dried herb (or two ounces of fresh) in a pint
of cool water in a saucepan. Bring the water to a boil, then
reduce the heat and let it simmer for 15 minutes to an hour,
depending on the herb. It's ready to use after straining the liquid and allowing it to cool. As with teas, decoctions are usually
drunk as a tea, but they may also be used externally as "washes"
or bathwater additives. In some cases they're used to soak a
cloth for use as a compress.

As with teas, decoctions are most effective right after brewing.
However, they can be stored in a sealed container in the refrigerator for up to 24 hours.

Herbal poultices. Poultices are generally used for external problems, such as wounds, sores, skin irritations, or swelling, or for painful areas caused by bruises, sprains, or arthritis. A poultice consists of a "mash" that can be created by crushing fresh herbs to a paste consistency, or by boiling dry herbs for 10 to 15 minutes. Another, perhaps less palatable, option is to do as Native Americans frequently did—chew the herb into a paste (without swallowing) and then apply it to the skin.

Regardless of how a poultice is prepared, it needs to be placed in good contact with the area being treated. This is usually done by applying the poultice directly to the skin, or by putting it between two pieces of thin cloth such as gauze, which makes the procedure tidier.

Some people are sensitive to certain herbs, and treated areas may redden or show other signs of irritation. This may mean an allergic reaction is occurring, so you should stop the treatment immediately.

HERBAL REMEDIES AND YOUR CHILD

If you are interested in trying any herbal remedy with your child, it's important to talk with your doctor first and consult an experienced herbalist about use and dosage. As with any medication, children can respond to herbs differently than adults; so you must exercise caution when administering any herbal treatment. The following chart can be used together with sound medical advice to prepare herbal teas for infants, children, and teens.

Recommended Doses of Herbal Teas for Children

AGE	DOSE
0–1 year	$\frac{1}{20}$ of the adult dose
1–2 years	$\frac{1}{10}$ of the adult dose
3–4 years	$\frac{1}{5}$ of the adult dose
5–6 years	$\frac{3}{10}$ of the adult dose
7–8 years	$\frac{2}{5}$ of the adult dose
9–10 years	$\frac{1}{2}$ of the adult dose
11–12 years	$\frac{3}{5}$ of the adult dose
13–14 years	$\frac{4}{5}$ of the adult dose
15 and older	Full adult dose

GATHERING HERBS

Native American herbalists received years of training before setting out on their own, and they worked in an environment that was free from pollutants—such as insecticides and chemical fertilizers—as well as from local ordinances. Modern Americans, however, have more to contend with, says herbalist Ana Nez Heatherley. A few safety precautions are essential.

- Picking any plant, including medicinal herbs, is illegal in some areas, so be sure you know the local laws before setting out.

- Don't harvest along busy highways or in other areas where there may be high levels of pollution.

- Always be sure you know exactly what you're gathering. Picking and using the wrong plant, Heatherley warns, is sure to do more harm than good.

- "Always think of the Earth and its well-being before taking any plant," she says. Harvest only from large groups of plants, and never take more than a third of those that are available. Don't take more than you plan to use, and do as little damage to the remaining plants and surrounding vegetation as possible. In other words, treat the environment with the same respect that Native Americans did.

DRYING AND STORING HERBS

Herbs are highly perishable even when dry, and will quickly lose their benefits unless they're properly prepared and stored.

Fresh herbs can lose potency in a matter of days, so most herbalists dry them for storage. To dry herbs, separate the leaves from the stems and spread them in loose, single layers on a clean, flat surface. Bulkier plants may be hung from a line in a dry area such as a warm basement or attic. Flies and other insects are sometimes attracted to herbs, so you may want to cover them with a layer of cheesecloth.

The time required for drying depends both on the herb and the environment in which it's being dried. Because herbs lose their potency so quickly, the shorter the drying period, the better. It usually takes about a week. An herb is sufficiently dry when it still has an aroma but is dry enough to break. If it crumbles completely when you handle it, you dried it too long.

Roots, which should be thoroughly washed before drying, take longer to dry than leaves and flowers—usually about three weeks.

Once they are dried, store them in glazed ceramic, dark glass, or metal containers with tight-fitting lids. Plastic bags or food storage containers will absorb the essential oils.

REMEDIES FOR COMMON AILMENTS

ACNE

An early Dutch explorer described the Native Americans as being "sound of body, well fed and without blemish." At a time when Europeans considered bathing harmful and skin was nowhere near as healthy as it is today, many observers marveled at the Native Americans' clear complexions.

Doctors now know that acne usually erupts when oil glands in the skin become blocked with cellular debris. When the pores can't drain, bacteria may gather inside, causing infection and inflammation. The best treatments for acne are often the simplest: good diet and hygiene, along with daily washing and astringent products for removing oils and bacteria.

It's doubtful that Native Americans worried much about their skin—but then, they routinely did things that helped keep it healthy and blemish-free. Here are their secrets.

Sweat it clean. The Native Americans gathered in sweat lodges for ceremonial rituals, but the intense steam and heat were good for their skin as well. Moist heat opens pores in the skin, allowing them to drain.

The easiest way to create your own "sweat lodge" is to luxuriate in the shower. With the bathroom door closed, run the water as hot as you comfortably can. To conserve energy, some people prefer to steam only their faces. You can do this by heating a pot of water on the stove until it comes to a boil. Remove from heat, then lean your face over the pot, draping a towel over your head to trap the steam. About 10 minutes of steam will open pores and help keep your skin healthy. Don't get too close to the hot water or the pot, however, or you could be scalded.

Use an herbal scrub. Washing your face at least once a day with a decoction made from healing herbs such as aloe, fennel, rose, sage, watercress, or yarrow will open the pores and help scrub away old oils. At the same time, herbal treatments help control the bacteria that can lead to acne.

To clean especially troublesome spots, herbalists recommend rubbing the area with fresh, crushed garlic. Garlic is a powerful bacteria fighter and will help prevent infections from getting started. Because of garlic's pungent odor, most people do garlic treatments at night, giving the skin a chance to "air out" before morning.

Cleanse your system. The health of the skin directly reflects the health of the whole body. Native Americans frequently drank herbal teas, using echinacea, dandelion, Oregon grape, stinging nettle, or goldenseal. Taken as often as three times a day, these teas help to remove harmful substances from the body's lymph system while strengthening the cleansing powers of the liver and kidneys. They also strengthen the immune system, helping the body fight harmful bacteria.

ANXIETY

Stress and anxiety are a way of life for most Americans today, but it wasn't always like this. Among the Native Americans, anxiety was rare, in part because they derived tremendous peace and comfort from their spiritual beliefs. As a 17th-century historian observed, "They have no law suits and take little pains to acquire the goods of this life, for which we Christians torment ourselves so much."

Life wasn't perfect for Native Americans, of course. During times of grief, famine, or war, they experienced tremendous amounts of stress, just as people do today. The difference is that they couldn't drive to the pharmacy to fill a prescription for the latest anxiety-soothing drug.

Fortunately, they didn't need to, because they were well versed in herbs that calm the mind and spirit. Scientists today have found that herbs such as dandelion, valerian, hops, black cohosh, rose, and goldenseal, usually taken as a tea several times a day, have naturally sedating qualities. If time and convenience are factors, you can buy these herbs as supplements or tinctures in health food stores.

One of the best healing herbs, rose petals, can be used externally to relieve anxiety. Herbalist Ana Nez Heatherley recommends running a bath and adding fresh rose petals to the water. To complete the experience, you can indulge yourself by drinking a cup of rose petal tea and maybe even hold a rose tea compress to your forehead. It won't be long before you're feeling "rosy" again.

ARTHRITIS

There are more than 100 kinds of arthritis, but the most common is osteoarthritis. Doctors estimate that about 16 million Americans have some form of osteoarthritis, which occurs when protective cartilage in the joints wears down, causing bone ends to grind against each other. Although injuries or certain diseases can also cause osteo-arthritis, it often results from nothing more than a lifetime of bending, lifting, and reaching. In fact, doctors often refer to it as "wear and tear" arthritis.

For the Native Americans, whose very survival depended on hard physical labor, arthritis could be a serious handicap. Not only does it produce pain and stiffness, but without treatment, it can cause the joints to become increasingly immobile. Native Americans were well aware of this risk, and they looked to nature for relief.

Try a sweat. Native Americans coped with arthritis flare-ups by spending time in the sweat lodge. You can get the same effect by closing the bathroom door and running the shower as hot as it will go. Sit nearby for 15 or 20 minutes to allow the heat and steam to penetrate the skin and loosen muscles, ligaments, and tendons. This will allow joints to move with less pain and stiffness.

Loosen your joints with water. Taking a long bath or shower is one of the quickest ways to get relief from arthritis flare-ups. The Native Americans knew this too, which is why they often retired to a sweat lodge or hot spring when their joints were acting up. Research has shown that moist heat increases circulation to painful areas. This allows the blood to bring in more healing nutrients and take away pain-causing toxins. At the same time, moist heat may encourage the body to produce naturally-occurring chemicals called endorphins, which have been called "natural morphine" because of their analgesic properties.

Ease the pain with willow. Willow bark contains a compound called salicin, which is very similar to the active ingredient in aspirin. When brewed as a tea, willow contains as much active painkiller as some modern analgesics. Adding a teaspoonful of dried licorice root to the tea will make it a little easier for the stomach to tolerate.

According to herbal authority James A. Duke, Ph.D., author of *The Green Pharmacy*, other teas that can relieve arthritis include black cohosh, poplar, and yarrow.

Counteract the pain with nettle. Scientists have found that a technique called "urtication," or deliberately irritating the skin, can make arthritis pain less severe. When you gently strike sore spots with a branch of stinging nettle, the tiny stingers inject small amounts of anti-inflammatory compounds. The idea isn't to damage the skin, but to strike it hard enough that you feel a slight irritation. This may be all it takes to relieve the arthritis flare-up.

Nettle can also be eaten as an arthritis remedy, according to Dr. Duke. It contains healthful amounts of the mineral boron, which has been shown to help ease arthritis. Cooking nettle softens the "stingers," but you'll want to wear gloves when preparing it.

ASTHMA

Asthma is nearly at epidemic proportions, especially among children. Doctors estimate that more than 14 million Americans have asthma, a condition in which airways in the lungs become constricted and inflamed. Narrowed airways cause wheezing and shortness of breath, and the inflammation results in the production of large amounts of mucus, which causes coughing and makes it even harder to breathe.

According to historical accounts, asthma appears to have been very rare among Native Americans. Part of the reason for this is probably environmental. Unlike people today, Native Americans weren't exposed to air pollution or crowded living conditions, both of which can lead to asthma. Also, even though they smoked ceremonially, they hardly had the pack-a-day habit that many Americans do.

In addition, Native Americans routinely used herbs that are now known to combat asthma. The various herbs act in different ways. Some are antispasmodics, which means they help relax the bronchial spasms that can trigger asthma attacks. Others are expectorants, which help remove phlegm from the lungs. Still others are sedatives, which reduce the emotional stress that is a common asthma "trigger."

Asthma can be a serious problem, so it's essential to work with a doctor before trying herbal remedies at home. Once asthma is under control, it's fine to add herbal teas to the treatment.

Herbalists advise attacking asthma with herbs from each of the three healing groups, using the following chart.

ANTISPASMODICS	EXPECTORANTS	SEDATIVES
black haw	garlic	black haw
milkweed	milkweed	mullein
valerian	mullein	valerian
garlic	peppermint	hops
fennel	licorice	lady's slipper
licorice		
peppermint		

BACK PAIN

It's hard to overemphasize the impact of back pain on Americans today. Doctors estimate that 80 percent of us will have back problems at some time in our lives, costing us not only in physical pain and emotional anguish, but also in billions of dollars of medical and other costs. Among Native Americans, however, back problems were relatively rare. This suggests that for everything we do that's wrong for our backs, they did something right.

The Native Americans were physically active, which means that their back and abdominal muscles were strong. They were rarely overweight and they experienced relatively little day-to-day stress, both of which play a role in keeping the back healthy. Even when they did get back pain, they knew exactly how to ensure that it didn't get worse. You may want to try a few of their secrets.

Heat it up. As devotees of the sweat lodge, Native Americans regularly exposed their backs to moist heat. Moist heat warms muscles so they stay loose and limber. It also increases circulation, which can flush pain-causing metabolic by-products from the lower back. Most Americans don't have sweat lodges, of course, but what we do have is even better because it's more convenient: a hot bath. Soaking in hot water at home or luxuriating in a whirlpool bath at the health club will quickly reduce back pain—and, more importantly, keep the muscles limber so there's less risk of back injuries later on.

Get a massage. Rubbing the muscles does more than loosen them up. It also may flush out pain-causing toxins such as lactic acid, which often contribute to back pain. According to historian Virgil J. Vogel, among the Cherokee, "The medicine man first warmed his hands over live coals, then rubbed the affected part in a circular motion with the right hand, most of the pressure being applied with the palm."

We can take advantage of the same technique today. Massage therapists are trained to understand how the muscles work and how to apply the appropriate pressure to relieve different kinds of pain. You can find a certified massage therapist by looking in the phone book—or ask your doctor for a recommendation.

Drink peppermint tea. Peppermint contains a compound called menthol, which has analgesic and muscle-relaxing properties. The easiest way to take peppermint is as a tea, which you can drink as often as needed to relieve pain.

Make a peppermint rub. Native Americans often rubbed sore muscles with a liniment made from peppermint. The menthol in the peppermint created a sensation of warmth that penetrated deep into the muscles. To make an herbal rub, loosely fill a jar with fresh peppermint leaves, add enough vegetable or mineral oil to cover the leaves, cap the jar, and store it in a cool, dark place, shaking it several times a day. After 10 days, strain off the oil and store it in a dark bottle. When back pain strikes, rub the oil thoroughly into the muscle for quick relief.

Or try sage. Like peppermint, sage can also be applied to the skin to help relieve back pain. To make a sage rub, mix a few drops of sage oil, available in health food stores and herb shops, with a couple tablespoons of vegetable oil. Dip your fingers in the oil and apply it to your back as often as needed.

Put willow to work. A popular pain-killer among Native Americans, willow works just as well as aspirin, but is somewhat gentler on the stomach, especially if you make a tea that also includes licorice root.

Stay as active as you can. Experts estimate that about 90 percent of back pain incidents could be avoided if we made a point of doing what the Native Americans did every day: exercise. Exercise strengthens the muscles in the back and abdomen, which in turn reduces the amount of daily pressure on the spine.

Exercise doesn't have to be formal or even especially rigorous to be beneficial. Walking is great exercise for preventing back pain. So is gardening. Trudging up and down stairs. Doing housework. As long as you're physically active, you'll naturally strengthen the muscles that are essential for protecting the back.

Here are a few additional tips for relieving and preventing back pain:

- Sitting is hard on the back, so it's important to get up and move around, even if it's just for a few minutes once an hour.

- If you spend a lot of time sitting, take the time to find a high-quality chair with good lumbar (lower back) support.

- Keep your back straight as much as possible. Even if you're merely picking up a sock from the floor, bend your knees rather than your back.

- When lifting, try to keep your back and legs in alignment. Twisting the torso when lifting is very hard on the back.

- Sleeping on a firm mattress provides additional support for the lower back, which can help prevent problems later on.

BAD BREATH

When historian John Lawson wrote in 1714 that the Native Americans he met around North Carolina were "among the sweetest people in the world," he wasn't just talking about their dispositions. Along with many other observers of the time, Lawson noticed that, compared to Europeans, the Native Americans were downright fragrant. Not only did they take frequent baths, but their healthful diets, combined with good dental hygiene, kept their breath fresh as well.

Bad breath is usually caused by bacteria that accumulate on the teeth, tongue, and gums. The Native Americans frequently used herbs that helped control bacteria and also had sweet, fresh-smelling flavors. According to herbal authority James A. Duke, Ph.D., some of these remedies worked better than the store-bought products we use today.

Chew on fennel or cardamom. The seeds of both herbs are pleasantly fragrant and naturally freshen the breath. In addition, they contain a bacteria-killing compound called cineole, which helps prevent smelly bacteria from accumulating. Chew the seeds thoroughly and either swallow them or spit out the shells once the flavor has been exhausted.

Eat some parsley. This fresh, grassy-tasting herb is a great source of chlorophyll, the same ingredient that's used in many breath mints, says Dr. Duke.

Gargle with peppermint or sage. Both of these sweet-smelling herbs have antibacterial properties. The leaves are a little too strong to eat, but they're great for making tea for gargling. You can gargle with the tea just as you would with a store-bought mouthwash.

BRUISES

Given their physically active lifestyles, Native Americans suffered their share of bruises. Not surprisingly, they became quite proficient at treating them, usually with herbal preparations that continue to be used today.

Bruises are caused by injuries to small veins, called capillaries, located beneath the surface of the skin. When the capillaries rupture, blood leaks into the surrounding tissue. This results in the purplish discoloration of bruises. The same process also causes pain and swelling because the body responds to the injury by releasing "scavenger" cells that are designed to remove debris from around the injury. These cells, along with a flood of fluids and other naturally-occurring chemicals, are what make bruises swell and ache.

Along with applying heat, Native Americans treated bruises with herbs that have analgesic, anti-inflammatory, and capillary-repairing powers. Here are some you may want to try.

Stop swelling with plantain. This herb contains potent anti-inflammatory compounds and is most often used as a poultice. Mash fresh plantain leaves, mix in a small amount of water, and apply the paste directly to the bruised area. A somewhat neater way to use plantain is to wrap the mashed leaves in a layer of cheesecloth and apply that to the skin.

Use mullein lotion. Like plantain, mullein is a powerful anti-inflammatory. It's most effective when applied to bruises as an oil-based lotion. To make the lotion, put a handful of mullein flowers in a jar, cover with olive oil, and allow to soak for 1 week to 10 days. Then strain out the flowers and apply the oil to the bruises. The oil will keep in the refrigerator as long as you store it in a covered, light-proof container.

Ease the discomfort with juniper. This aromatic plant was a favorite among Native Americans for soothing bruises. The easiest way to use juniper is to warm the branches slightly and attach them, using gauze or first aid tape, to the bruised area.

Reduce discoloration with parsley. When applied as a poultice, parsley will clear up most black-and-blue marks within a day or two, says herbal authority James A. Duke, Ph.D. To make a poultice, mash some fresh leaves and apply them directly to the skin— or wrap the poultice in cheesecloth, which is a little less messy.

Heal them with arnica. This popular bruise remedy can be applied externally as a poultice or compress, or taken internally as a tea, says herbalist David Hoffmann. To make a poultice, crush the leaves and hold them against the bruise. For a compress, make a strong tea, let it cool to slightly above room temperature, soak a cloth in the liquid, and apply it to the bruise.

Strengthen capillaries with yarrow. Taken regularly, this herb makes the capillaries more resistant to injuries, Hoffmann says. You can apply yarrow externally by making a compress from freshly brewed yarrow tea—or you can simply drink the tea.

Eat more fruits and vegetables. Foods that are high in vitamin C, like oranges, kale, and winter squash, can protect against bruises because this nutrient helps strengthen capillary walls.

Add some warmth. Native Americans believed that applying gentle heat to the skin was among the best remedies for helping bruises heal. Although heat shouldn't be used until a day or two after a bruise occurs (ice is better in the early stages), it can then be very effective because it improves circulation and helps flush fluids and debris from the area, says dermatologist Jerome Litt, M.D., of the Western Reserve University School of Medicine in Cleveland. He recommends applying a warm compress to the area several times a day for about 20 minutes each time. In most cases, this will help the discoloration fade more quickly.

BURNS

Burns have been the bane of mankind since the discovery of fire, and certainly the Native Americans weren't immune. Burns can range from superficial first-degree burns, in which only the outermost layer of skin is damaged, to more serious second- and third-degree burns, in which deeper layers of tissue are damaged. Any serious burn must be treated by a physician, especially if it covers an area larger than the size of a quarter. First-degree burns, however, can be effectively treated with traditional remedies.

Speed healing with aloe. "It's my first choice for burns," says herbal expert James A. Duke, Ph.D. It's also easy to use. Break open one of the succulent leaves, squeeze out the gel, and apply it to the burn. Studies have shown that aloe can increase blood flow to injured tissues, reduce inflammation and pain, and help burns heal more quickly.

Reduce infections with plantain. Like aloe, plantain has been shown to help stop infections and inflammation. Crush some fresh leaves and apply the juices directly to the burn as a soothing lotion.

Protect it with garlic. Although garlic may sting when applied to a burn, it's a very powerful infection fighter and makes an excellent antiseptic. Crush a few cloves and apply the mash directly to the burn.

Another herb that can stop infection is onion. A close botanical cousin to garlic, onion will also block bacteria and help burns heal.

Strengthen immunity with echinacea. Usually taken as a tea or tincture, echinacea gives the immune system a boost, making it better able to stop infections that may result from burns. You can also use echinacea externally as an antiseptic by applying the tea directly to the burn.

COLIC

Parents know the signs all too well: babies with colic, a condition caused by intestinal gas and spasms in the digestive tract, will cry incessantly, sometimes for hours, and their abdomens seem "tense" and bloated.

Native Americans had many remedies for colic, such as massaging the abdomen or applying a mud made from red clay. In most cases, however, they treated colic with herbs. Peppermint and fennel were two popular remedies, and they have the most research in their corner. As babies can't be given adult doses of herbs, use the conversion chart on page 127 for proper amounts.

Aid digestion with peppermint. Helpful for nearly all digestive complaints, peppermint can relieve colic by relaxing muscular spasms in the digestive tract. It also kills germs that may be causing some of the discomfort, according to herbal expert Daniel B. Mowrey, Ph.D. It can be given to babies as a very mild tea. (See the chart on page 127 for recommended doses.)

Stop discomfort with fennel. This pleasant tasting herb was popular among Native Americans because it had a calming effect on digestion. As with peppermint, it can be given as a mild tea to relieve colic in babies. (See the chart on page 127 for recommended doses.)

COLDS

It's not known how often the Native Americans suffered from colds, but in today's congested world, where we exchange sneezes as often as handshakes, the yearly average for adults is two to three colds a year. Children are much more vulnerable, averaging nine colds a year.

Scientists have been looking for cures for the common cold for hundreds of years. So far, however, they've been unsuccessful, so it's worth taking a lesson from the Native Americans. They weren't able to cure colds either, but they did have a number of remedies that could shorten a cold's duration and help the body recover more quickly.

Build immunity with echinacea. This herb was impressing Native Americans long before it began impressing scientists with laboratory findings. Research has shown that echinacea makes the immune system work more efficiently against cold viruses and a variety of other germs. It's most effective when taken as soon as cold symptoms begin, and may be used for as long as two weeks afterward.

Native Americans usually just chewed the roots of the echinacea plant, but the herb is just as effective as a tea, and most of all as a tincture. You can brew your own tea or try a commercially prepared echinacea tincture, using half a teaspoonful in a cup of water.

Don't be concerned if you notice a bit of tongue-tingling after drinking echinacea. That just means it's working.

Get comfortable with ginger. A favorite among Native Americans, ginger tea has been found to contain compounds that can help "neutralize" cold-causing viruses and also reduce pain and fever.

Relieve congestion with licorice. Known among Native Americans as an expectorant for clearing the lungs, licorice tea helps reduce the congestion that accompanies colds. Research has shown that licorice also increases the activity of a specialized component in the immune system, called interferon, which helps fight viruses.

Strengthen the spleen with goldenseal. This herb was a Native American mainstay. Goldenseal tea has been found to help the spleen, the organ that produces virus-fighting white blood cells, work more productively.

Stop viruses with garlic. This pungent herb contains a compound called allicin that has been shown to help block cold viruses. Another advantage of garlic is that its active ingredients travel directly to infected tissue in the lungs and respiratory tract when we breath, which puts the medicine right where it's needed, says herbal expert James A. Duke, Ph.D.

Garlic is most effective when it's eaten raw. A clove or two a day will go a long way toward keeping you healthy—or you can make a garlic tea by mashing several cloves of garlic and letting them steep in a cup of water for six to eight hours.

Lower fever with willow bark. Because willow tea contains active ingredients that are similar to those in aspirin, it can reduce fever as well as aches and pains. Do not give willow to children, however, as the aspirin-like compounds may increase the risk of a potentially serious neurological disorder called Reye's syndrome.

CONSTIPATION

Given what we now know about the effects of physical activity on staying regular, it's unlikely that constipation was a common problem among Native Americans. However, they must have had some problems with constipation because they invented the first-ever instrument for giving enemas. It was a syringe-like device, with the hollow leg bone of a bird at one end and the bladder of a small animal or fish at the other. Despite some technological improvements, enemas are given in much the same way today.

Another Native American treatment for constipation was a chewing gum made from the resins of the balsam tree. This treatment made sense because chewing gum is known to help relax the bowels due to the increased production of saliva, which contains digestive enzymes and can act as a lubricant. They had many other herbal remedies for constipation as well, a few of which are still used today.

Take herbal fiber. Researchers have found that dietary fiber is the best treatment for constipation because it absorbs water in the large intestine. This makes stools larger, which stimulates the intestines to move them along more quickly and easily. One of the best sources of fiber is seeds from the plantain plant. The psyllium absorbs tremendous amounts of water, making it one of the best remedies you can find.

To make a psyllium laxative, add a teaspoonful of plantain seeds to a cup of boiling water, allow to cool, then drink, seeds and all, once or twice a day. Be sure to drink a lot of water when using psyllium because it removes a lot of water from the body.

Some people are sensitive to the effects of psyllium, notes herbal authority James A. Duke, Ph.D. If psyllium makes you uncomfortable, you can get similar effects by eating more high-fiber foods, such as whole grains, fruits, vegetables, and beans.

Another herb that's high in fiber is flaxseed. It doesn't dissolve in water the way psyllium does, so rather than mixing it in liquid, it's best to add it to foods such as cereals or homemade breads. Take one to three tablespoons a day, and drink plenty of water, Dr. Duke advises.

Stimulate the intestines. You don't want to use it too often, but rhubarb root is a powerful laxative that stimulates the intestines. To use rhubarb, puree three stalks in the blender, being sure to remove the leaves, which are toxic. Add a cup of apple juice, a teaspoonful of lemon juice, and a tablespoonful of honey, and drink it once a day. But take heed: "Its laxative action can be pretty powerful," Dr. Duke warns.

COUGHS

At one time, many cough drops contained licorice, an herb that soothes the throat and helps act as a cough suppressant. Native Americans were fully aware of the powers of licorice. They often chewed the root, although in some cases they made licorice teas.

Other herbal teas that help relieve coughs include mullein, stinging nettle, magnolia, sassafras, honeysuckle, red clover, and the bark from trees such as balsam, pine, wild cherry, and birch. When making bark tea, you need to boil the bark for 15 minutes to release the active ingredients.

Although teas are effective, a more soothing strategy is to make an herbal syrup, which lingers longer on irritated tissues in the throat. Herbalist Ana Nez Heatherley recommends the following recipes.

Red Clover Cough Syrup

Ingredients
- 1 ounce fresh (or one-half ounce dried) red clover flowers
- 1 cup hot water
- 2 cups sugar

Place the ingredients in a saucepan and bring to a boil. Reduce the heat, simmer for 10 to 15 minutes, then strain the liquid and pour it into a glass jar with a tight-fitting lid. Cap immediately and store in a cool, dark place or in the refrigerator. Take one teaspoonful as needed.

Mullein-Honeysuckle Cough Syrup

Ingredients
- 1 tablespoon fresh (or 1 teaspoon dried) honeysuckle flowers
- 1 tablespoon fresh (or 1 teaspoon dried) mullein leaves
- 2 cups honey

Place the ingredients in a saucepan and bring to a boil. Reduce the heat and simmer slowly for 20 minutes. Strain the liquid and pour it into a jar with a tight-fitting lid. Store the syrup in a cool, dark place or in the refrigerator. Take one teaspoonful as needed.

DEPRESSION

Historians tell us that Native Americans were generally a high-spirited people, uplifted by their faith in the benevolence of Mother Earth and all her creations, plants and animals alike. This is the same resilient spirit that Native American psychotherapist Robert Blackwolf Jones tries to instill in his patients when they're feeling down. "Look at Mother Earth," he tells them. "All her birds sing. All her trees sway. All her waters splash. She lives with the strong heartbeat of life."

We should all strive to live so joyously, but when it's simply not possible, we can also look to Mother Earth for help.

Some types of depression are too serious to treat on your own. It's important to talk with a counselor or physician if you are experiencing sadness that just won't go away, feelings of hopelessness or worthlessness, changes in eating or sleeping habits, or suicidal thoughts. Most of the time, however, depression isn't this serious, and a mild case of "the blues" can be lifted with nature's help.

The Native Americans believed that keeping their bodies in peak condition would naturally brighten the emotions as well. With a combination of regular exercise, good nutrition, and the occasional use of mood-elevating herbs, they were able to keep their spirits high even when life brought them low.

There are many herbs that can affect mood, but here are the most common and well-studied.

Licorice root. St. John's wort has been getting a lot of attention lately as being "nature's Prozac," but licorice, which was commonly used by Native Americans, is thought by many herbalists to be just as important. "No plant has more anti-depressant compounds than licorice," according to herbal authority James A. Duke, Ph.D. "At least eight licorice compounds are monoamine oxidase inhibitors, which are compounds capable of potent anti-depressant action."

To get the benefits of licorice, drink up to three cups of licorice tea a day, brewed fresh or made by adding licorice tincture to a cup of hot water.

Caution: Licorice can have a toxic effect when taken for an extended period of time, so you should consider it a short-term remedy only—especially if you have high blood pressure or heart problems.

Purslane. "A whopping 16 percent of this herb consists of anti-depressive nutrients when measured on a dry-weight basis," says Dr. Duke. Purslane contains magnesium, potassium, calcium, folate, and lithium, all of which have anti-depressant effects. The best way to use purslane is as a salad green.

Oats. According to herbalist David Winston, oats are rich in the "nerve-fortifying" nutrients calcium, magnesium, and B vitamins. Oats, he says, can "soothe the frayed feeling of burning the candle at both ends." If you don't care for oatmeal, you can make an oat tea.

Scented herbs. Rosemary and sweet clover were used by Native Americans because they believed their pleasant aromas could help raise the spirits. Herbalists recommend hanging small bundles of these sweet-smelling aromatics around the house or in your office.

DIARRHEA

For all their health and vigor, the Native Americans did suffer from one malady at least as often as their European contemporaries, and that was diarrhea. Unclean drinking water often was the cause but, as with other ailments, the Native Americans were ahead of their time in concocting cures. In addition to using a wide variety of herbal teas, they used a drink made from the pulverized ashes of the fir tree—a remedy that makes sense because it's similar to the use of activated charcoal today.

There are many traditional remedies for this uncomfortable complaint, remedies that have been shown to be just as effective today as they were centuries ago.

Firm things up with teas. The first treatments Native Americans turned to for stopping diarrhea were herbal teas. Teas contain compounds called tannins. Tannins have been shown to constrict the walls of the intestines, thus limiting what they excrete. They also reduce the ability of the intestines to reabsorb things that may have caused the diarrhea in the first place, such as bacteria, viruses, or parasites.

Herbs traditionally used to stop diarrhea include raspberry, peppermint, goldenseal, and yarrow leaves. Helpful barks include oak, willow, magnolia, wild cherry, hawthorn, and dogwood.

Take extra fluids. Diarrhea removes a lot of water from the body, which can quickly lead to dehydration, especially in children. Drinking teas will help replace fluids the diarrhea takes out. It's also a good idea to drink extra water, clear broth, or fruit juices. Avoid carbonated drinks because the gas bubbles can increase the discomfort of diarrhea.

Add bulk with psyllium. Even though psyllium is often recommended for constipation, it works just as well to relieve diarrhea. Psyllium, which are seeds from the plantain plant, absorb water in the large intestine, which makes stools firmer. To prepare psyllium, add a teaspoonful of seeds to a cup of boiling water. Let it steep for 15 minutes, then drink it down, seeds and all, once or twice a day.

Avoid foods. Native Americans customarily restricted their food intake when diarrhea struck. Doctors today continue to recommend this approach. When the intestines are "out of sorts," you can give them a rest by going on a temporary fast for a day or two. Remember to take fluids or clear broth in the meantime, however.

EARACHE

Earaches are incredibly common, especially among young children. Doctors estimate that 80 percent of children will suffer some form of ear infection by the age of five. Earaches are often caused by an infection of the middle ear, although in some cases a buildup of earwax or a damaged eardrum may be responsible.

Native Americans had numerous ways of coping with earache, and many have stood the test of time. Here are a few you may want to try.

Soothe the ear with mullein. When earaches are caused by infection or irritation of the outer part of the ear, you can give relief by using an oil made with mullein. This herb acts as an antiseptic, killing bacteria while also soothing the delicate tissues, says herbalist David Hoffmann.

You can buy mullein oil in health food and herb stores—or you can make your own in advance. Put several tablespoons of finely chopped mullein leaves into a glass container, add olive oil to cover, seal the container, and store it in a warm place (such as on a sunny window sill) for two to three weeks, shaking it once a day. Then strain the oil into a dark glass container, seal it well, and store it in a cool, dark place.

Treat the earache by putting several drops of the oil into the ear. Seal the ear with a cotton ball for a while to prevent the oil from leaking out, Hoffmann advises.

Stop infections with garlic. "Dripping garlic oil directly into the ear canal has been shown to treat fungal infections as well as or even better than pharmaceutical drugs," reports herbal expert James A. Duke, Ph.D. You can make garlic oil at home, but many herbalists recommend buying it ready-made at health food stores or herb shops. Garlic is such a powerful germ fighter, in fact, that it's also effective when taken in the diet, Dr. Duke adds.

Stop infection from the inside out. Because most earaches are caused by infection, one of the best ways to stop them is to strengthen the immune system so it's better able to resist bacteria and other germs. Hoffmann recommends using teas made with echinacea, goldenseal, yarrow, or peppermint. When giving teas to children, be sure to use the proper doses. See the dosing chart on page 127.

Try an ear-soothing pillow. Native Americans sometimes treated earaches by sleeping on a small pouch filled with dried hops blossoms. If you don't have a pouch, cheesecloth works just as well. For extra comfort, wrap the hops in the cheesecloth and heat briefly in the microwave until it's pleasantly warm. Then hold it against the ear until you're feeling better.

FATIGUE

Exhaustion has become a national problem. Millions of Americans say they feel tired nearly all the time. Along with fatigue come a lot of physical and emotional problems, including headaches, difficulty concentrating, depression, upset stomachs, sore muscles and joints, reduced sexual desire, and even memory loss.

Was chronic fatigue a problem for Native Americans? Medical historians say no. Native Americans lived active, spiritually meaningful lives, and went to sleep and arose with the sun—a far cry from the hectic lives many of us lead today.

Part of the problem is that Americans are working longer hours than ever before. We leave the house early in the morning to go to stress-filled jobs, and often don't return until late at night. More and more people report working evenings and weekends just to keep up. Then there are all the emotional stresses—paying the mortgage, taking care of children or aging parents, and keeping the house in order. Basically, we don't get enough sleep to recharge our batteries, and even when we do sleep we often trudge through the day feeling exhausted.

It's a challenge for most of us, of course, to return to a much simpler way of living. However, many of the secrets of the Native Americans can still be used today to quickly restore lost energy.

Take one day at a time. That may sound like a cliché, but it really goes to the heart of the Native American philosophy and way of life. Many Native American tribes lived day-to-day because the demands of daily survival gave them little choice. It was a difficult life in many ways, but because they were focused on the here and now, they didn't burn all their energy worrying about tomorrow.

Modern Americans would do well to take a lesson from this. Because we're not coping with daily survival, we have the "luxury" of worrying about things in the future. We often feel overwhelmed by things we can't predict and may not be able to do anything about, according to David Sheridan, Professor in the Department of Preventive Medicine at the University of South Carolina School of Medicine.

It's not easy for people today to let go of long-term worries and focus instead on the moment, but it's worth trying, says Dr. Sheridan. Living life as though every day on Earth were your last makes it possible to see what's really important. At the same time, it allows you to concentrate your energy on things that make the biggest difference right now. When you take care of the details, says Dr. Sheridan, the bigger issues often take care of themselves, and this can leave you with much more energy than you had before.

Exercise lightly and often. In the last few years, more and more Americans have begun taking up exercise—and nearly just as many will give it up. The problem with "formal" exercise is that unless you really like biking, lifting weights, or what-have-you, it's hard to stick with it. A better approach, experts believe, is simply to incorporate physical activity throughout your day. That's what the Native Americans did, and their health and vigor proved it works.

An active lifestyle (as opposed to a formal exercise plan) merely means keeping your body moving. This can be as simple as walking to the store on the corner instead of driving. Taking the stairs instead of the elevator. Raking the yard instead of hiring a neighborhood teen to do it. Even if you're only physically active for a total of 30 minutes a day, your metabolism will run faster all day long and you'll rediscover the energy you'd forgotten you had. As a bonus, experts have found you don't have to get your exercise all at once for it to be effective. Staying active for 10 minutes at a time, and repeating it three times a day, is just as effective as exercising in a 30-minute block.

Sleep regular hours. Sure, it's easier said than done, but it's worth making the effort to get more shut-eye. Americans today don't get anywhere near enough sleep. We stay up late to watch TV, work at the computer, or tackle paperwork, but the alarm rings just as early the next morning. We try to "catch up" on weekends, but the body just doesn't work that way.

In some ways it was a lot easier for Native Americans to get enough sleep than it is for us. They didn't have electricity, cordless phones, or teenagers with drivers' licenses to worry about. The end of their day was marked by the setting of the sun, and sleep just came naturally.

We would do well to follow their example more closely. At the very least, we should try to be consistent in the amount of sleep we get, says exercise physiologist William Fink of Ball State

University. For most people, this means six to eight hours of sleep, not just during the week, and not just when it's convenient, but all of the time. If we would commit to sleeping regular hours, we'd find that our energy levels would naturally climb.

Regardless of how much you sleep at night, you may find that daytime naps are a great way to regenerate your energy, too. Unfortunately, most Americans are reluctant to nap because they feel they're not being productive enough—but the body really isn't designed to sleep only at night. Napping is one of the best ways to give your body the rest it needs, says Rick Rice, M.D., Professor of Family Medicine at Ohio State University. Native Americans did it all the time.

Take time to eat well. As part of our usual time crunch, we often forget how important it is to eat well. Fast food may be convenient, but it doesn't give your body everything it needs to perform at peak capacity, and snacktime sweets high in sugar can leave you feeling tired and sluggish. This is another area in which Native Americans were way ahead of us. They ate a very nutritious diet, filled with whole grains, beans, and small amounts of lean meat. Doctors have found that when people switch to a more "natural" diet, they often report feeling more energetic.

Go hot and cold. Native Americans amazed early European settlers with their custom of taking hot steam baths followed by a plunge into an icy river or lake. It was invigorating, to say the least.

Centuries later, a Bavarian herbalist, Sebastian Kneipp, perfected the technique and achieved worldwide fame for using this technique as a treatment for recurrent fatigue.

Unlike the Native Americans, you don't have to construct a sweat lodge or live in the woods to practice hot-and-cold treatments. All you have to do is take a long, hot shower, followed by an invigorating cold splash. You'll discover for yourself how quickly your energy levels can climb, and you may find that they stay elevated for hours afterward.

Try the energizing herbs. Research has shown that a number of herbs that Native Americans used to increase energy actually increase the body's metabolism. According to Daniel B. Mowrey, Ph.D., author of *The Scientific Validation of Herbal Medicine*, ginseng, ginger, and peppermint, taken separately or together as a tea, can quickly jump-start energy and reduce fatigue. You can brew fresh tea or use herbal tinctures or supplements, available in health food stores.

FEVER

A fever is often one of the first signs that you're getting sick. It's not a pleasant feeling, which is why most people do everything possible to lower fevers as quickly as possible. Getting your temperature down to 98.6 degrees will make you feel better right away. However, feelings can be deceptive. When you're sick and have a mild fever, lowering it is about the worst thing you can do.

Bacteria and viruses can only survive at certain temperatures. The fever you get when you're sick isn't part of the illness; it's part of your body's defense. "By heating itself up, the body slows down the growth of invading organisms," explains John C. Roers, M.D., of the Department of Family Medicine at Baylor College of Medicine in Houston.

Native Americans understood the importance of fever. Not only did they often let fevers run their course, sometimes they made things hotter by sending feverish people into sweat lodges. In a way, the sweat lodge was nothing more than a room-sized "fever."

Doctors today are unlikely to send patients with fevers into steam rooms. It's not that they disagree with the principle. It's just that most people wouldn't be willing to do it. So a compromise has been reached. Doctors usually recommend letting a fever run its course as long as it's under 103 degrees. Higher temperatures, or any fever that lasts longer than 48 hours, should be checked out by a doctor.

However, to beat mild infections and low fevers, it's worth taking a hint from Native Americans. They used herbs called diaphoretics that raised the body temperature just enough to give the immune system an extra boost. According to herbalist David Hoffmann, these herbs aid "the body's own innate recuperative powers."

Herbs that are recommended for fever include cayenne, ginger, sage, peppermint, boneset, goldenseal, milkweed, hops, rose, honeysuckle, and yarrow. These herbs are best taken as teas, which serves the double purpose of keeping the body hydrated while washing out the very germs they kill. Add a teaspoon of dried herb (two teaspoons if fresh) to a cup of boiling water. Allow to steep for 15 minutes, strain, and drink up to three cups daily.

To lower a fever, Native Americans used willow bark, which contains salicin, a fever-reducing compound similar to the active ingredient in aspirin. Just steep a teaspoon or so in a cup of boiling water for 15 minutes, strain, and drink as needed.

Caution: Because willow bark contains compounds similar to those in aspirin, don't give it to children, as it may increase the risk of a potentially serious neurological disorder called Reye's syndrome.

FLATULENCE

Intestinal gas has been around a lot longer than the bean burrito. It probably started about the time humans started eating carbohydrates, which is to say, with their very first meal. Gas usually results from the fermentation in the small intestine of two particular carbohydrates, raffinose and stachyose. The body doesn't have the digestive enzymes to break them down, so they linger in the intestine, fermenting and producing gas.

Some of the most healthful foods, unfortunately, contain these carbohydrates. Beans head the list, but cabbage, broccoli, brussels sprouts, onions, cauliflower, whole wheat flour, and bananas are close behind.

Normal flatulence isn't a medical problem. (In some cases, gas is a symptom of other conditions, so you should see your doctor if you're also having serious abdominal pain or pain that lasts longer than three days.) The average adult has been estimated to pass gas between 8 and 20 times an hour, so it's hardly unusual.

However, it can be uncomfortable, as well as embarrassing. Native Americans dealt with painful episodes in several ways: by massaging the abdomen, ingesting the powdered ashes of the fir tree, and taking what are known as carminatives—herbs that relax the muscles of the digestive tract and help gas escape.

The best Native American herbs for relieving gas pains are fennel, peppermint, sage, licorice, goldenseal, wormwood, dandelion, and yarrow. You can use any one of these herbs as a tea, taken up to three times a day.

GUM DISEASE

Doctors estimate that more than one third of Americans will develop gum disease by the time they're 20 years old, and more than half will have it by age 50. Gum disease occurs when bacteria in the mouth colonize a thin, invisible film called plaque that accumulates on the surfaces of the teeth. You can't see plaque or the bacteria it contains, but you'll see the signs in the form of red, irritated gums or bad breath that never seems to sweeten.

Gum disease, which is called gingivitis in its milder forms and pyorrhea when severe, can weaken the teeth as well as cause bad breath, says Robert Schallhorn, D.D.S., former president of the American Academy of Periodontology. Untreated, it's a serious problem, but it never has to go that far. It's among the easiest conditions to treat yourself, and Native American remedies are among the best. The proof is that Native Americans rarely got gum disease. In part, this is because they ate a lot of tooth- and gum-scrubbing raw vegetables, which acted like little toothbrushes every time they ate. In addition, they used herbs that they knew would keep their mouths healthy.

Put bloodroot to work. A potent herb called bloodroot is among the best herbs for dental health, says herbal expert James A. Duke, Ph.D. It's somewhat scarce today, but one of its active ingredients, an antibacterial compound called sanguinarine, is not. In fact, it's used in many toothpastes and mouthwashes and has been shown to help reduce plaque in as few as eight days.

Chew some protection. Native Americans didn't have WaterPiks, but they did have herbal "toothbrushes." One way they kept their teeth clean was by chewing on raw licorice roots. Not only is the root slightly abrasive, it also contains large amounts of an antibacterial compound called glycyrrhizin. Drinking or rinsing your mouth with licorice tea can also be effective, says Dr. Duke.

Other teas that are good for the gums and teeth include peppermint, stinging nettle, echinacea, watercress, and sage, all of which have antibacterial properties, says Dr. Duke.

Get the right nutrients. Because Native Americans lived close to nature, they always ate a lot of vegetables, grains, and other healthful foods. It's a good thing they did, because research suggests that certain nutritional deficiencies, especially deficiencies of vitamin C and magnesium, may result in gum problems.

To get healthful amounts of these nutrients, Dr. Duke recommends making a brew of dandelion, purslane, and stinging nettle.

HEADACHES

Some Native American remedies for headaches sound more suited to causing than curing one. Some tribes, for example, believed in curing headaches by holding bundles of skunk cabbage against the head. Others used poultices made of crushed pine needles, and an analgesic rub was made from petroleum oil, essentially the same goo you feed your car. Needless to say, Native Americans, like millions of people today, were desperate for relief.

Fortunately, there were better options available, many of which are still in use. Here are the best.

Relieve the pain with heat. About 90 percent of headaches belong to a category called tension headaches. This doesn't mean they're caused by stress, although stress may be involved. Tension headaches are caused by tense muscles in the shoulders and neck. The best way to relieve this type of headache is to relax the muscles, and applications of heat do just that.

Native Americans luxuriated in sweat lodges when they needed a dose of warm, moist heat. Today, you can get the same effect by holding a hot water bottle or a hot, moist towel against the tight muscles—or you can run a hot shower or bath and let the water work directly where it hurts.

Put your mind at ease. Research has shown that emotional stress and tension are responsible for a great many headaches, not only tension headaches but migraines as well. If you frequently get headaches, it's worth doing all you can to dispel some of the stress in your life. "What helps to keep them much in health is the harmony that prevails among them," wrote one 17th-century observer of the Native Americans.

Take an herbal cure. The Native Americans had a cornucopia of herbal remedies for treating headaches. Some herbs stopped the pain itself, whereas others helped reduce emotional stress and tension. Herbal teas recommended for easing pain include willow, peppermint, goldenrod, violet, rose, lavender, and sage. Vervain tea is a mild sedative and can help relieve headaches caused by stress.

Stop migraines with feverfew. This herb wasn't commonly used among Native Americans, but it's received tremendous attention from scientists, who believe it can stop migraines as well as some medications do. According to herbal authority James A. Duke, Ph.D., "Feverfew works for about two-thirds of those who use it consistently."

The editors of The Harvard Medical School Health Letter report similarly encouraging results. "Some people for whom conventional treatments for migraine have not worked have turned to feverfew with good results," they write.

You can chew feverfew leaves or use them to make a tea. A more convenient way to take feverfew is to use supplements, available in health food stores.

Don't take feverfew if you're pregnant because it can increase the risk of miscarriage.

HEMORRHOIDS

Few people like talking about them, and fewer still admit to having them, but according to Yale gastroenterologist Howard Spiro, M.D., hemorrhoids are as common as gray hair, "though somewhat more painful."

Doctors estimate that 75 million Americans, about one third of the population, have hemorrhoids. Best described as varicose veins of the anus, hemorrhoids occur when blood pools inside the blood vessels, causing them to swell. The majority of hemorrhoids occur inside the anus, where there aren't any nerve endings. Those that occur farther out, however, can be excruciatingly painful.

Hemorrhoids often accompany constipation, because straining to have a bowel movement puts pressure on the anal veins, causing damage that leads to hemorrhoids. Even when hemorrhoids don't hurt, they still make themselves known because they bleed, sometimes copiously. The unwelcome sight of blood in the toilet bowl gets many people to a doctor in a hurry. You don't want to ignore such sightings because bleeding may also be a sign of several other, more serious conditions. In most cases, the bleeding is caused by hemorrhoids, but it's important to get checked out to be sure.

Most hemorrhoids will go away on their own and don't cause serious problems. The exception is a hemorrhoid that becomes blocked by a blood clot. Although these aren't serious either, they can be incredibly painful, and sufferers will try almost anything for relief.

Native Americans had some innovative ways of dealing with hemorrhoids. One technique was to plug the anus with a suppository made from the bark of the dogwood tree. A more pleasant approach was to apply soothing poultices of mullein and goldenseal. Enemas were also used, some of which included a concoction made from witch hazel. Today, witch hazel is still the key ingredient in Tucks, a popular cleansing product for hemorrhoids. Witch hazel is an astringent, which means it causes blood vessels to constrict. This may be an effective way to stop hemorrhoids from bleeding and to reduce painful swelling.

Try putting a teaspoonful of dried witch hazel in a cup of boiling water. Let it steep for 10 to 15 minutes, then, when it's cool, soak a piece of gauze and apply it to the tender spots.

Herbalists today feel it makes more sense to stop hemorrhoids from the inside out, mainly by using herbs that relieve the constipation that causes them in the first place. According to herbal expert James A. Duke, Ph.D., the best Native American herb for easing constipation is psyllium. You can buy psyllium seeds in health food stores and herb shops. Add a teaspoonful of seeds to a cup of water and let them soak for about 10 minutes. Then drink the liquid as well as the seeds.

HIGH BLOOD PRESSURE

High blood pressure is known as a "silent killer." That's because there are few symptoms, no pain, and you can have it for years unaware. But all the while, it's damaging blood vessels and possibly the heart. That's why it's worth doing everything you can to keep blood pressure at healthful levels.

Medical historians believe that high blood pressure was rare among Native Americans. They did virtually everything that doctors today recommend to their patients. They kept lean and were physically active. They ate plenty of fresh fruits and vegetables and almost no salt—and, they were at peace with themselves and their environment.

As a bonus, many of the herbs they used all the time, such as black cohosh, garlic, onions, ginseng, plantain, purslane, saw palmetto, corn, honeysuckle, hawthorn, and yarrow, are now known to lower blood pressure. When blood pressure is low, the risk for heart disease and stroke is lowered, too.

High blood pressure is always serious, so you'll need to check with your doctor before treating yourself with herbs. If you get the green light, and in most cases you will, you can try any and all of these herbs. Some, like garlic, onions, purslane, and corn, are tasty foods that you can simply eat more of. Others you may want to take in supplement form—or you can brew herbal teas, drinking one to three cups a day. You may see measurable results in as little as a few months.

Also keep in mind the Native American low-pressure lifestyle. Current research has shown that lifestyle factors play an enormous role in causing, or reversing, high blood pressure. Among the most important things you can do are to keep your weight in a healthy range, stay physically active, limit the amount of salt in your diet, and discover how to control emotional stress.

It sounds like a rigorous program, but only because we're not used to thinking this way. For the Native Americans, who lived naturally and simply, it was very easy indeed.

"Free yourself," advises Robert Blackwolf Jones, a Native American psychotherapist. "Find the courage to be yourself, not a clone, not an expectation, not a programmed robot. A deer in the woods does not stare at the bear and wish it were a bear. It is fully content being itself."

INDIGESTION

You may remember the antacid commercial about the gentleman who couldn't believe he "ate the whole thing." You can be sure that Native Americans had similar moments. Because their food supplies could be uncertain, they sometimes went a little overboard during times of plenty.

How did they spell relief? With herbs that helped the digestive system work a little more efficiently, and also with remedies that simply helped them feel a little better.

One remedy, which may sound bizarre, was to mix the earth from beneath a campfire with water, boil it, strain it, add a touch of salt, and down the hatch it went. No one's been willing to personally test it, but researchers suggest this "cure" actually may have been effective because the charcoal-infused ashes could have neutralized excess acid in the stomach.

A more palatable remedy for discomfort caused by over-eating is to drink a tea made from goldenseal, ginger, or wormwood, according to herbalist David Hoffmann. Each of these herbs can neutralize stomach acid and also stimulate muscular contractions in the intestines, which makes digestion work more efficiently.

Because overeating often causes belching or flatulence, you may want to take a tea containing peppermint or fennel, both of which help reduce the buildup of gas in the digestive tract.

Finally, because emotional stress is a common cause of indigestion, you may want to take a tea that's mildly sedating, such as hops, valerian, chamomile, lavender, or rosemary, Hoffmann says.

INFLAMMATION

You sprain your ankle and suddenly it's twice its normal size—or you bruise your knee and the next day your leg looks like a python that swallowed a rabbit. Even a splinter in your thumb can cause it to double its girth. What's causing all this swelling?

It's just the body taking care of business. Whenever you get injured, the body responds by flooding the bloodstream with specialized cells and chemicals whose job it is to remove debris, attack germs, and generally try to patch things up. In the process, however, large amounts of fluids travel to the site of the injury. This is what causes swelling and inflammation, both of which can irritate nearby nerves. And that causes pain.

Because inflammation isn't responsible for healing, but is only a side effect of the process, you can take steps to limit it without interfering with your body's ability to heal. This is something Native Americans learned very quickly because, given the rigors of their lifestyles, they were in frequent danger of injury.

When inflammation was severe, they would sometimes puncture the swollen area, which allowed blood and fluids to drain out. A less dramatic remedy, and one that was often just as effective, was to put a poultice on the area—or they would drink teas that helped stop inflammation internally. Here are two remedies you may want to try.

Draw out the fluids. The principle of using a poultice is that certain herbs have the ability to draw fluids to the surface, allowing them to drain. In addition, some poultices release helpful compounds into the bloodstream. For sprains and bruises, Native Americans applied crushed leaves of witch hazel. Witch hazel contains anti-inflammatory compounds that can help reduce swelling. (You can buy bottled witch hazel in supermarkets and pharmacies.) Other anti-inflammatory poultices contained crushed pine bark, purslane, plantain, corn, yarrow, and tobacco.

Stop inflammation from the inside. For some kinds of swelling, especially swelling caused by arthritis, Native Americans often used anti-inflammatory teas made with ginger, willow, or dandelion. As with poultices, these herbal teas are loaded with anti-inflammatory compounds, says herbalist James A. Duke, Ph.D.

INSECT BITES

For us, insects are an occasional nuisance, but for the Native Americans they were a way of life. Living face-to-face with nature, often sleeping with nothing but pine needles beneath them and the stars above, they undoubtedly were viewed as "dinner" by more than a few hungry members of the insect world. They didn't have commercial repellents like we do, but they did discover ways to make themselves a little less desirable to hungry insects.

Repel them with herbs. One way Native Americans avoided close encounters of the biting kind was to cover themselves with bear oil. A more attractive remedy today is pennyroyal, a member of the mint family. You can crush pennyroyal leaves and rub the juice on exposed skin. Hanging dried pennyroyal plants in your home can also repel insects.

Soothe the sting. To ease the discomfort of insect bites and stings, Native Americans would apply a poultice made from mullein, plantain, echinacea, onion, and garlic. For serious bites, they would suck the affected area to remove as much venom as possible, followed by an application of a soothing herb.

These remedies may sound primitive, but there's good evidence that they worked, says James Duke. He has found, for example, that rubbing your skin and clothes with any member of the mint family makes a very effective repellent. If you do get bitten or stung, go ahead and use a poultice made with any of the herbs the Native Americans used. Poultices can help reduce pain and swelling. They're most effective when used right after the bite or sting occurs.

INSOMNIA

The sleepless night has to rank among our worst nightmares, and certainly among our most common. In a recent survey of over 1,000 adults, one-third said they routinely had trouble falling asleep.

It's not known to what degree Native Americans had similar problems getting enough quality shut-eye, but they developed a number of remedies to aid in sleep. Here are a few you may want to try.

Calm yourself with herbs. To help your mind and body prepare for sleep, herbalists recommend taking a calming tea, made with hops, lady's slipper, vervain, or willow shortly before bedtime.

Have a relaxing soak. Another way to use herbs is to add them to bathwater, says herbalist David Hoffmann. He recommends adding two handfuls of dried herb (or four handfuls of fresh) to three cups of boiling water. Let the water stand for 30 minutes, strain, then add the liquid to bathwater. As the medicinal compounds in herbs are absorbed through the skin, they can create a sense of "full-body" calming, Hoffmann says.

ITCHY SKIN

The Native Americans had a lot of experience with itching. They lived in a wild environment, filled with insects, harsh weather, and allergy-causing pollens. They didn't have antihistamines or calamine lotion, so they had to find their own ways of getting relief.

Try an herb soother. Perhaps the quickest way to stop itching is to brew an herbal wash, using witch hazel, goldenseal, licorice root, echinacea, comfrey, or chamomile, and apply it directly to the skin or as a wet compress.

Calm the skin with oats. Native Americans didn't have the luxury of bathtubs. If they had, you can be sure they would have tried what many herbalists recommend today: taking an herbal bath by adding a couple handfuls of breakfast oatmeal to the bathwater. A neater alternative is to wrap oatmeal in cheese-cloth or tie it in an old cut-off stocking and drop it into the tub.

Cleanse the system. Itching isn't always caused by external factors. Conditions such as eczema and psoriasis can create almost unbearable itching. (For more on these conditions, see page 182-183.) To give yourself an "internal" scratch, you may want to try a tea made from Native American herbs such as echinacea, dandelion, yellow dock, stinging nettle, licorice root, burdock, or red clover. These herbs help cleanse the blood of bacteria and toxins that may contribute to these conditions, says herbal authority Daniel Mowrey, Ph.D.

Care for your skin. Dry skin often causes itching, so it's essential to keep it moisturized, especially in winter when the air is dry, says Hillard Pearlstein, M.D., a dermatologist at Mount Sinai School of Medicine in New York. Native Americans took care of this by rubbing their skin with bear or mountain lion oil. Today, there are less gamey options, and any commercial moisturizer will work well, Dr. Pearlstein says.

It's best to apply moisturizers right after bathing to help lock in the moisture, he notes.

MEMORY LOSS

More people than ever before are living into their 80s and 90s, and that's a good thing. However, along with aging come a host of age-related maladies, none more feared than memory loss.

Nearly half of people 85 and older suffer from some type of memory-robbing disorder—and nearly everyone loses at least some of their memory as they get older.

Experts still don't know what causes Alzheimer's disease, but research suggests that a number of Native American herbal remedies may have helped protect them. Native Americans prized these herbs for their ability to impart mental clarity, so perhaps it's more than a coincidence that they're the same ones scientists now believe show promise for stopping Alzheimer's.

Bee balm. Also called horsebalm and horsemint, this herb contains two important compounds, carvacrol and thymol, which research suggests may play a role in preventing the onset of Alzheimer's disease. You can take it as a tea, using fresh or dried herbs. Because some herbalists report that these compounds can be absorbed through the scalp, you may want to add a few drops of tincture to your shampoo.

Peppermint. According to herbal expert Daniel Mowrey, Ph.D., this popular Native American herb "prevents congestion of the blood supply to the brain, stimulates circulation and strengthens and calms the nerves." Research has shown that college students taking peppermint may score higher on examinations, Dr. Mowrey reports.

Ginseng. Well-known for promoting energy and mental alertness, ginseng may help improve the flow of blood to the brain, which could help with memory, says Dr. Mowrey.

Sage. As far back as the 17th century, sage was believed to improve memory or a "weak brain." Scientists believe it may provide help in the battle against Alzheimer's because it's thought to prevent the breakdown of an important brain chemical called acetylcholine.

Willow. Studies have shown that people who take anti-inflammatory drugs such as aspirin have a lower risk of developing Alzheimer's disease. Because willow contains an active ingredient similar to that in aspirin, it may also be helpful.

Dandelion. In laboratory studies, dandelion has been shown to improve the memories of mice, reports herbalist James A. Duke, Ph.D. Researchers suspect this is due to its high concentrations of lecithin, a compound which, like sage, may slow the breakdown of acetylcholine.

Stinging nettle. This plant is high in boron, a mineral that can boost levels of estrogen in the body, says Dr. Duke. Higher levels of estrogen have been shown to improve short-term memory in several studies.

Dandelion can be eaten fresh, but the other memory-enhancing herbs are best taken as a tea.

MENOPAUSAL PROBLEMS

Many women sail through menopause without a hitch, but others aren't so lucky. As estrogen levels decline, some women experience symptoms ranging from headaches and hot flashes to vaginal dryness. Today, women having difficulty with menopause can find relief with supplemental estrogen. However, Native Americans had to find their own remedies. They looked, as always, to nature to find them—and they were highly motivated to succeed.

Unlike many cultures, Native Americans had tremendous respect for women of all ages. It was their custom to hold women "in the highest regard," says Robert Blackwolf Jones, a Native American psychotherapist. Why else, he explains, would the force of creation itself be called Mother Earth?

This may explain why the Native Americans developed an enormous number of herbal remedies for treating problems associated with menopause. They created so many, in fact, that herbalist Amanda McQuade Crawford devoted an entire book, *The Herbal Menopause Book*, to the topic. Here are the ones researchers believe hold the most promise.

Black cohosh. This herb has been found to contain estrogen-like substances that may help relieve many symptoms of menopause, including hot flashes and vaginal dryness.

Licorice. Like black cohosh, licorice contains estrogen-like compounds. It also has a compound called glycyrrhizin, which appears to act as a natural regulator, raising estrogen levels when they're low and lowering them when they're high.

Red clover. Rich in estrogen-like isoflavones, red clover has been found to promote estrogenic activity.

Boron-rich foods. The mineral boron can help increase estrogen levels in the body, according to herbal expert James A. Duke, Ph.D. Foods that are high in boron include strawberries, peaches, cabbage, tomatoes, dandelion greens, apples, asparagus, figs, poppy seeds, broccoli, pears, cherries, beets, apricots, currants, parsley, cumin seed, and dill.

MENSTRUAL PAIN

Each month, a woman's uterus builds up a lining that is nature's way of "preparing the soil" should a pregnancy occur the following month. During menstruation, the uterus contracts to shed that uterine lining. For many women, the accompanying cramps are bothersome, but not especially painful. However, for others, especially young women, cramping can be severe.

Painful menstruation was occasionally treated by holding a hot compress to the abdomen, much as women use hot water bottles today. The main remedies, however, were herbal teas. "Everything from first menstruation to menopause was treated herbally, and there are many plants that do a great job in this area," says herbalist Douglas Shar, author of *Backyard Medicine Chest*.

Foremost among the herbal remedies was black haw. It was so effective at relieving menstrual cramps that colonial physicians sometimes used it also to reduce the muscular contractions associated with miscarriage. An herb called squaw vine, which was sometimes combined with raspberry leaves, was also effective.

NAUSEA AND VOMITING

No matter how unpleasant, vomiting is a protective mechanism that allows the body to get rid of whatever's making it sick. That's why doctors often say that the best treatment for nausea is to let it run its course.

This isn't always true, however. Some types of nausea, such as those caused by pregnancy or motion sickness, have no useful purpose—nor does vomiting that continues after the stomach has been emptied. These bouts of nausea should always be stopped.

The Native Americans didn't have planes or cars, so motion sickness was unlikely to be a problem. However, they were just as susceptible to other types of nausea, and they developed quite a few helpful remedies.

Ease nausea with ginger. According to herbal expert Daniel B. Mowrey, Ph.D., ginger tea is better for preventing nausea than modern over-the-counter drugs. If you're planning a trip, he says, it's best to take ginger prior to embarking; it's much more effective at preventing nausea than stopping it once it begins.

You can also use ginger tea to reduce nausea that occurs during pregnancy or when you have the flu. Ginger supplements, available in health food stores, are also very effective.

Soothe your stomach with peppermint. Usually taken as a tea, this herb is well-known for reducing gastric spasms that can lead to nausea. Don't drink more than a few cups if you're pregnant because large amounts of peppermint can increase the risk of miscarriage.

Browse the herbal menu. Native Americans used many different herbs for relieving nausea. An herbal tea that doesn't work for one person might very well work for another, so it's good to keep your options open. Herbs you may want to try include licorice root, goldenseal, chamomile, black horehound, blackberry leaves, lemon balm, and fennel.

PROSTATE ENLARGEMENT

Every man has a prostate gland, and by the age of 50 half have an enlarged prostate gland.

The prostate gland is responsible for supplying the fluid that makes up semen. It's shaped like a doughnut and it wraps around the urethra (the tube that carries urine) near the base of the bladder. When the prostate gland swells, a condition called prostatic hypertrophy, it may begin pushing inward against the urethra, making urination slow or difficult. It some cases, it swells outward and presses against the large intestine, interfering with the passage of stools.

Doctors sometimes use drugs to reverse the swelling, but the medications aren't ideal because they can have sex-inhibiting side effects. Fortunately, there are other alternatives. Problems with the prostate gland weren't unheard of among Native Americans, and they developed a number of remedies that are still in use today. One of these remedies, in fact, may offer a bonus by providing a sexual lift.

Saw palmetto. The Seminole tribe in the Southeast first discovered this small palm tree, and they nibbled the seeds as a food. It wasn't long before they noticed that it was helping older men with prostate problems as well.

"Its benefits include increased urinary flow, reduced residual urine, and decreased frequency of urination," says Purdue University Professor of Pharmacognosy, Varro Tyler, Ph.D. In a German study of over 2,000 men, researchers found that a daily dose of one to two grams of saw palmetto seeds (the equivalent of about 320 milligrams of saw palmetto extract) produced substantial improvement.

Saw palmetto appears to reverse prostatic swelling by preventing the male hormone testosterone from being converted into a compound called dihydrotestosterone, which is thought to be responsible for prostate growth. Because of saw palmetto's reputation for increasing sex drive, it's among the most popular herbal aphrodisiacs being sold today. Most people take saw palmetto in supplement form.

Pumpkin seeds, licorice root, and stinging nettle. Each of these herbs, which were widely used by Native Americans, has captured the attention of researchers for its potential prostate-shrinking powers. As with saw palmetto, they are believed to work by preventing testosterone from making a prostate-enlarging conversion to dihydrotestosterone.

Pumpkin seeds can be roasted and eaten whole. Licorice root and stinging nettle are usually taken as teas.

Prostate enlargement can be a serious problem, not only in its own right, but because some of its symptoms may be similar to those caused by prostate cancer. To rule that out, it's important to call a doctor at the first sign of symptoms, the most common being frequent or difficult urination.

SKIN CONDITIONS

Elizabeth Arden, eat your heart out. In addition to their physical prowess, the Native Americans were known for their smooth, clear complexions. Given the harshness of their environment, their fresh appearance was even more amazing.

According to one historian, Native Americans had great skin because they anointed their bodies with the oil of fish, and the fat of eagles and raccoons. Another observer credits their clear complexions to lotions made with bear oil and a variety of herbs.

There's no question that Native Americans treated their skin with ingredients we'd find less than appealing today. But they did more than smear on bear or eagle fat. They took great pride in their appearance, and used a variety of techniques to keep their skin fresh and young-looking and also to treat mild skin problems. People with eczema, for example, would use the fresh, top leaves of a yarrow plant as a skin rub and as a remedy for rashes. Some tribes are reported to have mixed egg whites with charcoal from the wood of the birch tree. According to an 18th century doctor impressed by this concoction's success, it was a "gallant remedy for cuts, wounds and scurfy sores upon the shins."

Let's take a look at how Native Americans treated some common skin problems.

CUTS AND ABRASIONS

Native Americans lived a rough, rugged lifestyle, and skin injuries were common. Fortunately, so were the remedies for treating them.

For minor cuts and abrasions, Native Americans from northern tribes applied the antiseptic resins of the balsam tree. Tribes farther south used antiseptics made by boiling the barks of birch and hemlock trees. Yet another popular remedy was the sap of the red elm. According to one European observer, it was good for "taking away scruff, pimples, spots and freckles from the face."

Although some of the remedies were quite intricate and required considerable preparation, you can obtain similar results with an antiseptic wash, which will prevent infection and help superficial wounds heal more quickly. To make the wash, add a teaspoonful of dried herb (echinacea, goldenseal, and witch hazel are good choices) to a cup of boiling water. Let it steep for 15 minutes, then strain and apply the liquid to the wound, either directly or by soaking a piece of cloth or gauze.

You can also prepare an antiseptic poultice by crushing garlic cloves or comfrey leaves and rubbing the paste directly on the cut or sore.

One of the best balms for minor cuts and scrapes is the gel from an aloe plant. Research has shown that aloe does more than soothe cuts. It can also help them heal more quickly. You can buy aloe preparations in health food stores and herb shops, but the best remedy is also the simplest: break off a stem from an aloe plant and squeeze it to extract the gel. Apply directly to cuts, scrapes, rashes, or minor burns.

ECZEMA

Doctors still don't know what causes this condition, which results in dry, flaky, itchy skin, but they do know what will soothe it. Some of the best remedies are also the oldest, commonly used by Native Americans centuries ago. The main treatment for eczema is to pump extra moisture into the skin. Most dermatologists agree that the best way to do this is to apply a moisturizer after taking a bath or shower. This will help trap moisture next to the skin so it can be absorbed, says dermatologist Bruce Bart, M.D. The moisturizer doesn't have to be fancy, he adds. Petroleum jelly or an inexpensive lotion works just fine.

During an eczema flare-up, you can soothe the skin and relieve the rash by using traditional Native American herbs. Herbalists believe that the best choices are oats (which can be used as a poultice or added to bathwater by the handful), licorice root (which can be drunk as a tea or applied to the skin as a wash), and watercress (also applied directly or drunk as a tea). Other herbs you may want to try, either as a tea or a skin wash, include goldenseal, stinging nettle, yellow dock, and red clover. You can also crush clover leaves and use them as a poultice to relieve itching, says herbalist Ana Nez Heatherley.

Psoriasis

Psoriasis is a mysterious condition in which skin cells develop 5 to 10 times faster than usual, resulting in thick, scaly patches. The problem with psoriasis isn't merely that it's unsightly; it's intensely itchy as well.

Some of the best ways to soothe the itch include taking cool baths to lubricate the skin, applying moisturizers, and getting lots of sunshine. Exposure to the sun is often the best strategy because in some cases it can clear the skin entirely, at least for a while. The problem with sun, of course, is that too much exposure can increase the risk of skin cancer. That's why you may want to try other, safer remedies first.

Many herbs commonly used in Native American healing appear to help people with psoriasis. Chamomile is one of the best. You can apply a chamomile compress to affected areas, or you can buy a chamomile lotion in health food stores. Licorice root, drunk as a tea or applied as a wash to the skin, is also helpful. In addition, many herbalists recommend adding several handfuls of breakfast oats to bathwater, which gives it a smooth, silky feeling.

It sound strange, but another helpful remedy is red pepper. Peppers contain a compound called capsaicin, which can help relieve the discomfort of many skin conditions. Rather than applying red peppers directly to the skin, doctors recommend using a capsaicin-containing ointment, available in pharmacies. The ointments are irritating at first, but most people report improvement within a few weeks.

People with sensitive skin may want to avoid these creams because in some cases they may make the discomfort worse.

POISON IVY

The bane of anyone who enjoys the great outdoors, poison ivy could be a real annoyance for Native Americans. The plant contains a powerful oil that can be intensely irritating when it touches the skin. What's more, the oil is extremely long-lasting, remaining active for months or even years. This means that even when people didn't touch poison ivy directly, they could still get a rash by touching something that once did, like clothing or a tool handle.

The Native Americans didn't waste time scratching; they came up with effective remedies for poison ivy. One of their favorites was impatiens, also known as jewelweed. The frail blossoms can be mashed and applied directly to the skin to stop itching. Other plants, including aloe, bearberry, willow, and sassafras are also helpful.

RINGWORM

A pesky fungal infection that causes a serious itch, ringworm can usually be subdued with skin washes made from

Native American herbs, such as echinacea, plantain, gold-enseal, licorice root, ginger, and yellow dock, all of which have been found to contain potent anti-fungal compounds. To make the wash, add a teaspoonful of dried herb (or two teaspoons of fresh) to a cup of boiling water. Let steep for 10 to 15 minutes, then strain and apply to the skin, either directly or as a compress.

In addition, you can use garlic as a rub to help arrest ringworm, and the milky sap of the milkweed plant has been shown to be effective.

SHINGLES

The problem with shingles is that the virus that causes it, a member of the herpes family, never goes away. After an attack it retreats into the body until one day it rises to the surface again, triggering a painful rash on the face or torso. Within a week or two, the rash turns into blisters similar to those caused by chicken pox.

There is no cure for shingles. The virus often burns itself out, but in the meantime all you can do is cope with the pain. Many herbalists report successfully treating the condition with strong skin washes made from the popular Native American herbs lemon balm, licorice root, and purslane, all of which are loaded with anti-viral compounds.

To make a wash, add a teaspoonful of dry herb (or two tea-spoons of fresh) to a cup of boiling water. Steep for 10 minutes, then strain and let cool. You can apply the washes directly to the skin or by using a wet compress.

Warts are benign tumors that can be caused by any one of 30 different viruses. As you might expect for such a common condition, there are nearly as many remedies as viruses. The Native Americans were surprisingly successful in treating warts, and the remedies they used work just as well today.

Willow or birch bark. Take a piece of bark, wet it, and tape it to the wart, with the inner side of the bark facing the skin. If you apply a new piece of bark each day, you should see results in about a week. An alternative is to apply a strong wash made by boiling the bark, says herbal expert James A. Duke, Ph.D.

Dandelion or milkweed sap. Break a leaf or stem and squeeze the milky liquid onto a wart. Repeat this several times a day until the wart is gone.

Some people are sensitive to wart treatments, and you'll need to discontinue the treatments if your skin gets sore or irritated, says Dr. Duke.

SORE THROAT

Sore throats are usually caused by colds and flu and will quickly respond to remedies for these conditions. (See page 144 for more information on treating colds and flu.) However, in some cases a sore throat may be caused by pollution, smoking, or even yelling or talking too much. Less often, a sore throat is produced by a bacteria called *streptococcus*, which must be treated by a doctor. Sore throats that are caused by infections will usually be accompanied by other symptoms, such as a fever or general aches and pains.

Native Americans had a number of remedies for soothing sore throats, but the most popular was herbal teas, which can be used both as a gargle and a drink. Repeat the treatments every few hours until your throat improves.

Some of the best teas for throat pain include echinacea, goldenrod, licorice root, pine needles, mullein, peppermint, rose petals, sage, slippery elm, and willow.

SPRAINS

Sprains aren't as serious as a broken bone, but you might not know it. They can be equally painful, sometimes taking weeks or even months to improve.

Sprains occur when tendons (which connect muscle to bone) or ligaments (which connect bone to bone) get stretched beyond their ability to bounce back. These tough, fibrous tissues are notoriously slow to heal. About the only thing that helps is to increase blood flow to the injured area, something the Native Americans learned to do in a variety of ways.

One of the best ways to help a sprain heal is to rub and massage the area. According to historian Virgil J. Vogel, the Cherokee were masters of massage, and this was probably their first choice for treating sprains. The Native Americans also knew the wisdom of immobilizing severe sprains. They often used wrappings of rawhide or splints made from tree branches and twigs. Soothing poultices made from warm red clay or anti-inflammatory herbs such as arnica, bearberry, mullein, yarrow, and wormwood also eased pain.

According to one European doctor, the Native Americans treated sprains and broken bones with a skill that "equaled and in some respects exceeded that of their white contemporaries."

Historians don't know the exact details of the Native American treatment for sprains. However, the herbalist David Hoffmann has developed a natural technique for easing sprains that he believes is very similar to that used by Native Americans, though most tribes may have used cold compresses, not ice.

• Apply ice to a sprain as soon after the injury as possible. Wrap the ice in a cloth or plastic bag to prevent damage to the skin and hold it against the sprain for about 20 minutes. This will constrict blood vessels and help reduce swelling later on.

• Bring a pint of water to a boil and add two ounces of rosemary or thyme, herbs that stimulate circulation. (Herbs such as bearberry, mullein, yarrow, wormwood, and arnica can also be used.) Let the mixture simmer for about 15 minutes, then set aside to cool. Soak a cloth in the solution and wrap it around the injured area. Change and resoak the dressing every four hours until the pain begins to subside.

• Once the pain subsides, soak a strip of gauze in witch hazel, available in pharmacies, and wrap it around the injured area.

In addition to treating sprains externally, it's also helpful to treat them from the inside with bearberry tea, drinking up to three cups a day.

VARICOSE VEINS

The body's veins are designed to collect "used" blood from tissues throughout the body and return it to the heart and lungs. To make sure blood always travels in the right direction, the veins are filled with tiny one-way valves. As columns of blood move through the veins, these valves snap shut behind them, preventing the blood from slipping backward.

It's an ingenious system, but it isn't always effective because the valves occasionally weaken and lose their strength. This often happens in the leg veins because the blood, affected by gravity, is harder to push upward. When the valves "slip," blood flows backward, forming pools of accumulated blood. Over time, more and more blood flows into these pools, causing the veins to swell. After a while the veins get so large or discolored that they become visible through the skin. These are known as varicose veins.

Doctors sometimes inject medicines that seal off the damaged veins, forcing blood to find other, more efficient routes. But there are also natural remedies that can help, two of which were commonly used by Native Americans.

According to herbal expert James A. Duke, Ph.D., eating raw violet flowers is probably the best place to begin. Violet flowers contain a compound called rutin, which has been shown to help fortify capillary walls. Eating several teaspoonsful of violet flowers a day (pansies may also be used) can make a real difference, says

Dr. Duke. Other natural remedies that may increase capillary strength include hawthorn berries and horse chestnuts.

There's some evidence that you can also strengthen veins from the outside by applying witch hazel, available as a liquid or tincture in pharmacies and health food stores, says Dr. Duke. Some herbalists believe that drinking witch hazel tea can also strengthen the veins.

These herbal treatments will be most effective when you're also eating a diet that's rich in fruits, vegetables, legumes, and whole grains. These foods are high in fiber, which, by preventing constipation and the attendant straining that increases pressure on blood vessels, can also help prevent varicose veins. Regular exercise makes a big difference, too, because moving the muscles also moves the veins, helping to thrust blood in the right direction.

WRINKLES

It's unlikely that facial wrinkles concerned the Native Americans much. After all, they had tremendous reverence for age, whereas people today are more likely to fight the aging process. They did care about appearance, however, and historians believe that they treated their skin with loving care.

Native Americans kept their skin meticulously clean and fresh with frequent sweats. They also made sure to moisturize and protect skin from the weather by using animal fats—bear fat, especially. And, of course, they used herbs, including purslane, witch hazel, rosemary, and sage.

Each of these herbs, scientists now know, are extremely good for the skin because they're rich in antioxidant compounds. Antioxidants help combat wrinkles by blocking the harmful effects of naturally occurring oxygen molecules, called free radicals, that are known to damage the skin.

The easiest way to use these skin-healthy herbs is to drink them as teas. You can also brew herbal teas and apply them to the skin as a compress—or do what many Native Americans did. Grind fresh leaves to a paste and apply them as a poultice.

Using these herbs as poultices can be especially effective because of their astringency. They tighten the skin by causing proteins within it to temporarily contract, explains herbal authority James A. Duke, Ph.D.

A facial made with purslane is particularly effective, he says. Run a handful of fresh purslane through the blender. Then dab the mash on your face, leave it on for 15 to 30 minutes, and rinse your face thoroughly.

YEAST INFECTIONS

We tend to think of yeast infections, known as candidiasis, as mainly a female problem affecting the vagina. However, any moist area of the body, including the mouth, anus, and even armpits, can harbor the yeast-like fungi called Candida. In the world of microorganisms, Candida is singularly adaptable. Yeast infections have been increasing in recent years because the

Candida fungus appears to thrive in people who are taking modern drugs, including birth control pills, steroids, and some antibiotics.

You need to see a doctor if you suspect you have a yeast infection. But even if you're taking anti-fungal medications, you can give healing an added boost with Native American remedies. A few of these are considered especially effective.

Echinacea. This herb stimulates the body's white blood cells, which can help destroy the organism causing the infection. You can either drink echinacea tea or apply it directly to the infected areas. As with many herbal remedies, echinacea is also available in supplement form.

Bearberry. This popular Native American herb contains a potent anti-fungal compound called arbutin, which is also present in cranberries and blueberries. Bearberry can be taken as a tea.

Cranberry juice. Along with cranberry sauce and fresh blueberries, adding extra cranberry juice to your diet can help combat yeast infections.

Goldenseal, goldenrod, and sage. Each of these herbs contains anti-fungal compounds. You can drink them as teas or apply them directly to the skin.

AFTERWORD

We'll never know exactly what motivated the first Native American who prepared willow bark to lower a fever, or how shamans discovered the health-giving benefits of massage, or what inspired some intrepid soul to flail himself with nettle to relieve the pain of arthritis. What we do know is that early Native Americans were deeply attracted to nature's mysterious forces and diligently studied the world around them.

They undoubtedly observed that birds, deer, and other animals ate certain plants only when they were sick—and taking their cue from the beasts, they tried these remedies themselves. Other discoveries must have been made by chance: a tea drunk for flavor was found to ease insomnia; smoky corn cobs in the fire seemed to stop itching; and delicately flavored fresh dandelion helped heal liver problems.

Native Americans didn't become expert healers overnight. Every discovery, the successes along with the failures, was passed along to succeeding generations. Even though they had little knowledge of science or the biological workings of the body, centuries of experimentation—what scientists today might call case studies—gave them the knowledge they needed to keep people healthy.

Their legacy lives on. Many of the remedies used by Native Americans centuries ago are still used today, not only by their descendants, but also by herbalists and physicians throughout the world. In some countries, in fact, herbal remedies are used as much as or more than modern drugs. Why? Because nature's cures have been shown to be safe and effective, and they often cause fewer side effects than modern drugs. And, as any doctor will tell you, that's good medicine.

NATIVE AMERICAN SACRED PLACES

The Native Americans revered the Earth and all her plants and animals as sacred. They also worshiped certain locations that they believed were endowed with special spiritual significance. These places included mountaintops, dense forests, springs, lakes, and waterfalls. Native Americans often visited these special places to perform religious ceremonies, search for spiritual guidance, or seek help in healing. According to Tom Cowan, author of *Shamanism as a Spiritual Practice for Everyday Life*, these places are "natural power spots where we feel our senses peaked and our consciousness lightened and raised."

Here we list some of the better-known places in the United States held sacred by Native Americans. To learn more about these and other locations, check with your local historical society. We thank Bernyce Barlow, author of Sacred Sites of the West, for her help in preparing the following information.

Oak Creek Canyon, Arizona, Slide Rock State Park. This site is considered one of the most powerful purification sites in the West. According to the Hopi Nation, the place has the ability to restore balance and drive out negative influences. Today, Native Americans continue to make yearly pilgrimages to the canyon for the same reasons. Oak Creek is said to bring harmony to those who bathe in its sacred waters.

Grimes Point, Nevada. Shamans of the Great Basin area used this site for ceremonies that would ensure a successful buffalo hunt by capturing the collective "soul" of the herd. They believed that the buffalo would come to the hunters in order to retrieve their souls.

Indian Hot Springs, Hudspeth County, Texas. Twenty-two artesian wells emerge from this sacred healing site, each with its own unique character and medicinal properties. One is a lithium spring, another is chemically similar to what we call Epsom salts. The mud from some of the springs was applied to the skin to cure rashes. Well-worn paths leading from spring to spring are still visible, reminders of how frequently the springs were sought for their healing powers in years gone by.

Moodus Cave, Mt. Tom, Connecticut. Used by the Wangunk tribe, this medicine site was the home of the spirit Hobomoko, who was believed to chase away evil spirits with his boisterous roar. Actually, the roaring sound was the result of earthquakes originating from the cave in a small area 4,560 feet beneath the surface. These quakes have been known to topple chimneys as far away as Boston and New York.

Eureka Springs, Arkansas. This site was revered as a place capable of curing blindness and eye afflictions of all types. So strong was this belief—based on the legend that here the eyes of the blind daughter of a Sioux chief were miraculously restored to sight—that the waters of the springs were used by Civil War soldiers in an effort to regain sight lost in battle.

Assateague Island, Maryland and Virginia Coasts. Used as a ceremonial healing site by many tribes of the eastern United States, the island was considered to be the East Coast portal for souls to enter and exist in this world. Point Conception in California was thought to be its western counterpart.

Fakahatchee Strand, Florida. A healing site for the Seminole Nation, this area is considered the home of God, the "Great Breathmaker." Like the vines that wrap around the cypress trees in this area of the Everglades, the Seminole believed that healing forces intertwined with the body when one visited this sacred place.

Lost Sea Cave, Sweetwater, Tennessee. This cave contains the largest underground lake in the world and is considered sacred by the Cherokee. They believe the cave is the home of an ancient spirit whose sympathy for humans is so great that anyone who bathes in the lake's sacred waters is healed in spirit, body, and mind.

Chimayo, New Mexico. The focal point of this site is a chapel, built in 1816, which is known as a place of miraculous healing events. On Good Friday of each year, thousands of people continue to come to the chapel at Chimayo looking for healing miracles. Many have allegedly occurred.

Mt. Shasta, California. This area has been used by tribes of the region as a place of purification and renewal for thousands of years. It was a popular spot for sweat lodge ceremonies and rituals designed to integrate body and mind. Vision quests often took place on Mt. Shasta. An area below it, known as Panther Meadows, was used for preparation and cleansing before the beginning of a quest.

Big Sur, California. Big Sur was thought to be a magical healing area by a tribe known as the Esalens. Shamans would use the Big Sur springs to wash away any disease residue that "stuck" to them after they performed healing on the sick. It was also believed that the places where the spring waters tumbled into the ocean were openings into the underworld, where shamans could enter to retrieve souls needing to be healed.

Ku-kui-haele and Wai-manu, Hawaii. These two sites were the original schools of healing for the *kahunas,* or tribal healers, of the Hawaiian Islands. They were founded by Lonopuha and his teacher Ka-maka-nui-'aha'i-lono (the white healer from "Land Far Away"), and are still considered sacred by Hawaiian healers today.

HERBAL SHOPPING GUIDE

Herbalist and Alchemist
51 South Wandling Avenue
Washington, NJ 07882
800-611-8235
Bulk herbs, herbal extracts, ointments, oils, and books.

Belmont Organics
5051 Biddeford
Comstock Park, MI 49321
616-784-9514
Website: www.herbsorganic.com
Email: belmont@herbsorganic.com
Organic herbs and herbal products.

Herbs and More
RR2 Box 202
Wewoka, OK 74884
405-257-5820
Specializing in medicinal herbs.

Vitamin Express
888-546-5667
Website: www.vitaminexpressway.com
*Herbs, herbal extracts, vitamins, minerals and
performance supplements.*

Jean's Herbal Tea Works
119 Sulphur Springs Road
Norway, NY 13416
888-845-TEAS
Website: www.jeansgreens.com/
Email: jean@jeansgreens.com
Specializing in medicinal herbal teas.

Glenbrook Farms Herbs and Such
15922 76th Street
Live Oak, FL 32060
888-716-7627
Website: www.herbs.genglo.com/
Specializing in nonirradiated herbs and herbal products.

Well-Sweep Herb Farm
317 Mt. Bethel Road
Port Murray, NJ 07865
908-852-5390
Specializing in high-quality herb plants.

Lingle's Herbs
2055 N. Lomina Avenue
Long Beach, CA 90815
800-708-0633
Website: www.linglesherbs.com
Specializing in organically grown herb plants.

Clear Meridian Dream
Website: www.meridian-dream.com/
*Herbal health care products, spiritual books,
and Native American products.*

Blessed Herbs
109 Barre Plains Road
Oakham, MA 01068
800-489-4372
Website: www.blessedherbs.com
Specializing in mail-order herbs.

Maitake Products, Inc.
222 Bergen Turnpike
Ridgefield Park, NJ 07660
800-747-7418
Website: www.maitake.com
Specializing in mail-order herbs.

Dry Creek Herb Farm
13935 Dry Creek Road
Auburn, CA 95602
530-878-2441
Organically grown herbs.

Native Essences
800-533-5511
Website: www.herbalalternatives.com
*Old Indian good-health herbal formula discovered by nurse Rene
Caisse, available in dry or tincture form.*

Terra Firma Botanicals
126 Sutherlin Lane
Eugene, OR 95405
541-485-7726
*Wildcrafted and other organic herbal products, fresh and dried
herbal extracts, flower oils, skin salves, massage oils.*

Weleda, Inc.
P.O. Box 249
Congers, NY 10920
800-241-1030
Website: usa.weleda.com
Calendula and other organic healing products, many for children.

INTERNET RESOURCES

The following Websites provide information on Native American healing practices. Be aware, however, that Websites change frequently—some sites may be discontinued, while others are being created all the time. With a little "Net-surfing," anyone interested in Native American healing should be able to find valuable information on the Internet.

Association of American Indian Physicians

http://www.aaip.com

Dedicated to excellence in Native American health care by promoting education in the medical disciplines, honoring traditional healing practices, and restoring the balance of mind, body, and spirit.

Dance of the Deer Foundation

Center for Shamanic Studies

http://www.shamanism.com

Information on shamanic health and healing, dreams, and visions.

Herb Dot Com

http://www.herb.com

News about herbal healing and source lists for approved herbs and health products.

Herbs for Health
http://herbsforhealth.miningco.com/msubamind.htm
A resource for Native American herbalism and practices. Contains links to a variety of related Websites.

Indian Health Service
http://www.ihs.gov
An agency of the U.S. Public Health Service, Department of Health and Human Services. Contains extensive information on the agency's goals and services and a listing of health care and administrative resources.

BIBLIOGRAPHY

Barlow, Bernyce. *Sacred Sites of the West*. Llewellyn Publications, 1996.

Bratman, Steven, M.D. *The Alternative Medicine Ratings Guide*. Prima Health, 1998.

Bruchac, Joseph. *The Native American Sweat Lodge*. The Crossing Press, 1997.

Carter, Forrest. *The Education of Little Tree*. University of New Mexico Press, 1976.

Cowan, Tom. *Shamanism as a Spiritual Practice for Everyday Life*. The Crossing Press, 1996.

Crawford, Amanda McQuade. *The Herbal Menopause Book*. The Crossing Press, 1996.

Deloria,Vine, Jr.. *Red Earth, White Lies*. Scribner, 1995.

Duke, James A., Ph.D. *The Green Pharmacy*. St. Martin's Paperbacks, 1997.

Georgakas, Dan. *The Broken Hoop*. Zenith Books, 1973.

Grimm, William C. *Indian Harvests*. McGraw-Hill, 1973.

Hartz, Paula R. *Native American Religions*. Facts On File, Inc., 1997.

Heatherley, Ana Nez. *Healing Plants: A Medicinal Guide to Native North American Plants and Herbs*. The Lyons Press, 1998.

Henry, Edna. *Native American Cookbook*. Julian Messner, 1983.

Hoffmann, David. *The Complete Illustrated Medicinal Herbal.* Element Books Limited, 1996.

—*The Herbal Handbook: A User's Guide to Medical Herbalism.* Healing Arts Press, 1987.

—*The New Holistic Herbal.* Element Books Limited, 1990.

Hutchens, Alma R. *A Handbook of Native American Herbs.* Shambhala Publications, 1992.

Jager, Mariah. *Alternative Healing Secrets.* Ottenheimer Publishers, Inc., 1998.

Jones, Robert Blackwolf and Gina Jones. *Listen to the Drum.* Commune-A-Key Publishing, 1995.

Kowalchik, Claire, Ed. *Rodale's Illustrated Encyclopedia of Herbs.* Rodale Press, 1988.

Lawson, John. *History of North Carolina.* 1714.

Lyon, William S. *Encyclopedia of Native American Healing.* W. W. Norton & Company, 1996.

Mehl-Madrona, Lewis, M.D. *Coyote Medicine.* Simon and Schuster, 1997.

Mowrey, Daniel B., Ph.D. *The Scientific Validation of Herbal Medicine.* Keats Publishing, Inc., 1986.

Ody, Penelope. *The Complete Medicinal Herbal.* DK Publishing, Inc., 1993.

Rockwell, David. *Giving Voice to the Bear.* Roberts Rinehart Publishers, 1991.

Shar, Douglas. *Backyard Medicine Chest: An Herbal Primer.* Elliot and Clark Publishers, 1995.

Verrill, A. Hyatt. *Foods America Gave the World.* L. C. Page and Company, 1937.

Vogel, Virgil J. *American Indian Medicine.* University of Oklahoma Press, 1970.

Weiss, Gaea and Shandor Weiss. *Growing and Using Healing Herbs.* Outlet, 1992.

Wolf, Fred Alan. *The Eagle's Quest.* Touchstone, 1991.

Writer Porter Shimer specializes in health, fitness, and psychology. He is the former executive editor of *Men's Health Newsletter* and *Body Bulletin* from Rodale Press, and has also worked as a journalist. His nationally syndicated column, "Bodyworks," appeared in newspapers across the country in the mid-1980s. He is also the author of *Keeping Fitness Simple, 55 Ways to Conquer Headaches, Body Shaping, More Fat-Burning Foods, Contagious Emotions,* and *Backache: 51 Ways to Stop the Pain.* His articles have been published in *Prevention, Reader's Digest, Ladies Home Journal, Men's Health, Runner's World, Healthy Woman,* and *Organic Gardening.*

Shimer is a graduate of Princeton University and lives in Emmaus, Pennsylvania.